Being Greek
The Culture of the People of Greece
2nd Edition

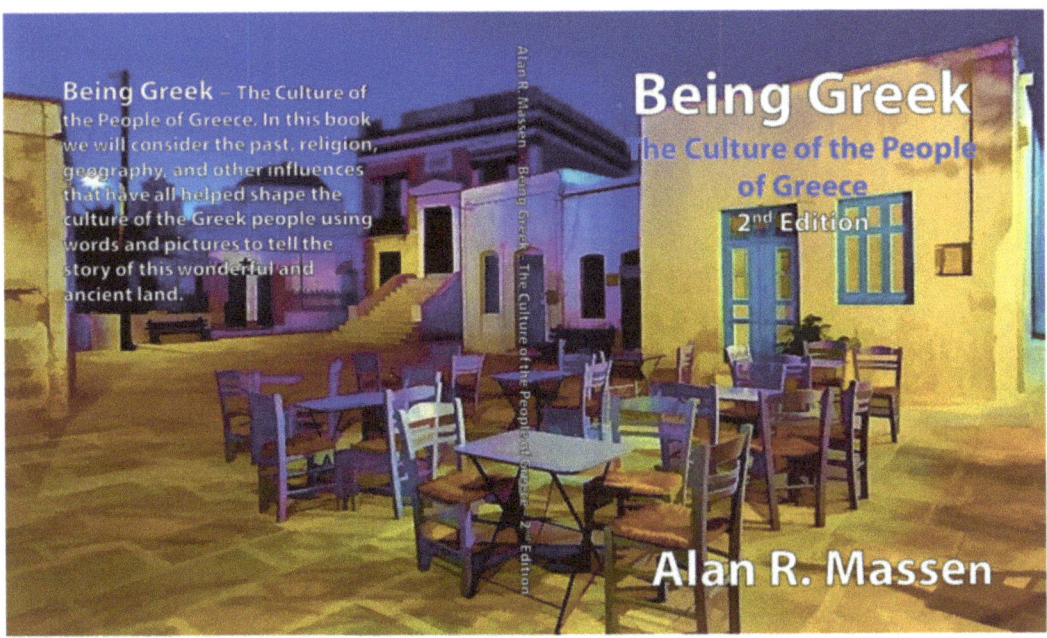

Being Greek – The Culture of the People of Greece. In this book we will consider the past, religion, geography, and other influences that have all helped shape the culture of the Greek people using words and pictures to tell the story of this wonderful land and it's people.

by Norfolk Watercolour Artist - Alan R. Massen
Published in Great Britain by Rainbow Publications UK

Books by the same Author

Retiring to the Garden Year 1 - Paperback
Retiring into a Rainbow - Paperback
Retiring into a Rainbow - Hardback
Retiring to our Garden Year one - 1st & 2nd Editions - Paperback
Retiring to our Garden Year two - 1st & 2nd Editions - Paperback
Retiring into a Rainbow - 1st & 2nd Editions - Paperback
Skiathos a Greek Island Paradise - 1st & 2nd Editions - Paperback
Norfolk the County of my Birth - 1st & 2nd Editions - Paperback
Art Inspired by a Rainbow - 1st & 2nd & 3rd Editions - Paperback
Ibiza Island of Dreams - 1st & 2nd Editions - Paperback
Majorca Island in the Sun - 1st & 2nd Editions - Paperback
Flip-Flops and Shades on Thassos - 1st & 2nd Editions - Paperback
Mardle and a Troshin' in Norfolk - 1st & 2nd Editions - Paperback
England the Country of my Birth - 1st & 2nd Editions - Paperback
Mousehole the Cornish Jewel - 1st & 2nd Editions - Paperback
Sunshades & Flip-Flops on Kefalonia - 1st & 2nd Editions - Paperback
Shades & Flip-Flops on Zakynthos - 1st & 2nd Editions - Paperback
Trips into my Minds Eye - 1st & & 2nd & 3rd Editions - Paperback
Corfu and Mainland Greece - 1st & 2nd Editions - Paperback
Crete and the Island of Santorini - 1st & 2nd Editions - Paperback
Cyprus - Pyramids - Holy Land - 1st & 2nd Editions - Paperback
Greek Islands in the Sun - 1st & 2nd Editions - Paperback
Being Greek - 1st & 2nd Editions - Paperback

E-books and Booklets:

Egypt - Land of the Pharaohs
Retiring to the Garden Yr 1 - Retiring into a Rainbow - My Art 1997 - 2018 - Skiathos a Greek Paradise Island
My Norfolk - My Greece - My England - My Team - My Skiathos - My Art - My Album - My Village
Greece Land of Gods and Men - Norfolk Wildlife - Civilisation (Empires of the Past)
Boudica Queen of the Iceni - Roman Britain - Norfolk by the Sea

Copyright © 2019 Alan R. Massen
Published in Great Britain by Rainbow Publications UK

First Published in 2018 by Rainbow Publications UK
2nd Edition Published in 2019 by Rainbow Publications UK

Copyright © 2019 Alan R. Massen

The moral right of Alan R. Massen to be identified as the author of this work has been asserted in accordance with the UK Copyright, Designs and Patents Act of 1988. All rights reserved.

No part of this book may be reproduced, or stored in a retrieval system, or transmitted in any form or by any means, electronic, mechanical, photocopying, recording, or otherwise, without the prior written permission of both the author and the above publisher of this book All imagery and illustrations

© Alan R. Massen

Neither the publisher nor the author can accept liability for the use of any of the materials, methods or information recommended in this book or for any consequences arising out of their use, nor can they be held responsible for any errors or omissions that may be found in the text or may occur at a future date as a result of changes in rules, laws or equipment All manufacturers, sellers, product names and services identified in this book are used in editorial fashion and for the benefit of such companies with no intention of any infringement of trademarks. No such use or the use of any trade name is intended to convey endorsement or other affiliation with this book

Paperback Edition ISBN 978-0-9935591-9-8
Typeset in Minion Pro
Published in Great Britain by Rainbow Publications UK

Dedication

We are the champions my friend!!!

I would like to dedicate this book to my football team Norwich City FC (the Canaries of Carrow Road, Norwich) who I have been supporting for more than sixty years. On Sunday 5th May 2019 Norwich City beat Aston Villa 2 - 1 away to finish Champions of the Championship and gain promotion back to the Premier League next season. In November 2019 I will be seventy years of age and I am so proud and excited that my team will be playing, against the big boys, once more in the top division of the English football league. On the Ball City - Come on you YELLOWS…

I would also like to dedicate this book to every member of my family and all of our good friends. A special mention must go to Evia, and George of the Mythos Cafe in Skiathos Town, Ervin, George, Yellis, Yannis and everyone else at the Troulos Bay Hotel on Skiathos and our good friends Karl, Anna, Issy, Alistair, Andrew and Lynn. A special thank you must also go to my wife Susie who accompanies me on all of life journeys. Last, but not lest, to all of the wonderful Greek people that we have met over the many years we have been visiting them and their beautiful Country and paradise Islands that we in the UK call Greece.

by Norfolk watercolour artist - Alan R. Massen.
Published by Rainbow Publications UK

About the Author

Alan was born in the city of Norwich in the county of Norfolk, England in November 1949. When Alan was still a teenager he started painting whilst attending art classes in Norwich. In his mid-teens he had two paintings accepted for a National Art Exhibition held in London and other major UK cities. Alan spent most of his working life as a professional Health and Safety Advisor and rarely picked up a paint brush until Alan, his wife Susie and daughter Ginny (his other daughter Mandy is married and lives with her husband Adrian in Sheffield) moved out of the city of Norwich into the countryside in 1993. They moved to a little village called East Lexham in the heart of Norfolk. The village was very peaceful and pretty. This helped inspire Alan to take up watercolour painting once again.

In 2004 they moved to another small West Norfolk village near Downham Market where they still live today. In 2008 Alan had to retire due to ill health (bad knees) and whilst he still painted regularly he began to spend more and more time gardening. In 2013 his wife Susie suggested that he kept a gardening diary to record his adventures in the garden and capture the changing seasons, animals, birds and the successes and failures of being a gardener he encountered. By the following year Susie suggested that he should write a book from his diary and include illustrations of both the garden and his artwork.

In 2014 Alan's first book was published by Creative Gateway called "Retiring to the Garden – Year One". This proved such a success that Alan decided to follow this up with his second book called "Retiring into a Rainbow" featuring his watercolour paintings. He then in 2015 published "Retiring to Our Garden – Year Two" published this time by Rainbow Publications UK. He then re-issued his first two books this time in a "Second Edition". Also published by Rainbow Publications UK.

In 2017 and 2018 he published the following books: "Skiathos a Greek Island Paradise", "Norfolk the County of my Birth", "Art Inspired by a Rainbow", "Ibiza Island of Dreams", "Majorca Island in the Sun", "Flip-flops and Shades on Thassos", "Mardle and a Troshin' in Norfolk", "England the Country of my Birth", "Mousehole the Cornish Jewel", "Sunshine and Shades on Kefalonia", "Shades and Flip-flops on Zakynthos" and finally "Trips into my Mind's Eye" Also published by Rainbow Publications UK..

In 2019, be starting on the following new books which will be entitled: "Trips into my Minds Eye - 2nd Edition", "Crete and the Island of Santorini", "Cyprus the Pyramids and the Holy Land", "Corfu and Mainland Greece", "Flip-flops and Shades on many Greek Islands" and finally "Greece Land of Gods and Men". When completed they will also be published by Rainbow Publications UK...

Contents

Introduction	1
The Gods of Greek Mythology	8
Ancient Greek History	35
The Ancient Sites of Greece	41
The History of Greece	69
The Religion of the Greeks	75
The Geography of Greece	83
The Greek Civilisation	96
The Economy of Greece	106
Greece at its Best	120
Being Greek	141
Greece in Colour	173
Acknowledgement	212

Copyright © 2019 Alan R. Massen

Introduction

Being Greek – The Culture of the People of Greece: In this book we will consider the ancient past, religion, geography, and other influences that have all helped shape the culture and beliefs of the Greek people using words and visual art to tell the story of this wonderful land and its people. Greece is a country located in south-east Europe located between the Mediterranean and Aegean Seas. The country of Greece includes many islands such as Rhodes, Crete, Corfu, Skiathos, Thassos, Kefalonia, Zakynthos to name but a few. The places that you could visit in Greece are endless as there is something to suit everyone with a wealth of historical sites, sporting venues, walking trails, museums, landmarks, monuments, festivals, carnivals, beaches and everywhere has great shopping opportunities. In this book, we will meet some of the ancient gods, visit many of the important archaeological sites and learn something about the history, geography and religious beliefs of the Greek people. Then we will visit some of the best beaches, towns and villages on the mainland of Greece and the Islands before reading about some of the beliefs of the people who make up the country that in the UK is called Greece…

Introduction:

Alan enjoying the sun…

In this book you will see numerous examples of my watercolour paintings and photographic artwork which I have scanned onto my computer. Then using a piece of art software, to give the pictures an impressionist style finish, a bit like Claude Monet, to produce the illustrations used throughout this book. So if you are ready we will start our journey together. I thought, that first I ought to introduce myself for those of you that have not read one of my other books in which I journey to visit the Greek mainland and many of the Greek Islands. Hello my name is Alan and I am married to Susie, we live in Norfolk in the UK and together in the last twenty five years, we have had numerous summer holidays abroad. Our holiday destination of choice, over the years, has usually been to go to one of the many Greek Islands. We have, over the years, holidayed on the Greek Islands of Corfu, Ithaca, Crete, Zakynthos, Santorini, Thassos, Kefalonia and Skiathos to name but a few. We have also visited many of the major archaeological sites on the mainland of Greece as well as spending several days visiting the important archaeological sites in the Greek capital of Athens. So now you know who I am let us return to the introduction of:

Being Greek – The Culture of the People of Greece …

Introduction:

Susie and I love Greece. It is full of warm hearted people, wonderful locations, a great climate and health giving foods such as fresh fish, vegetables, fruit, wine, feta cheese and of course olives. In this book we will be visiting many of the valleys, mountains, monasteries, forests, flowers, animals, olive trees, coastline villages, towns and beautiful beaches of this paradise country. Greece, is surrounded by crystal clear blue azure Mediterranean, Aegean and Ionian Seas. It benefits from having a relaxing warm Mediterranean climate which makes it an ideal place to visit. We have, over the years, stayed in many of its mainland cities, towns and villages and enjoyed every moment. We have also visited and/or stayed on many of the Greek Islands including Skiathos, Corfu, Crete, Kefalonia, Ithaca, Paros, Paxos, Santorini, Skopelos, Thassos and Zakynthos to name but a few. One of the best things about holidaying in Greece is the great Greek food. We even enjoy having Greek food at home. Susie uses olive oil, feta cheese and fresh olives in many of her meat and fish recipes and dishes to give us the great taste of Greece on our plate…

Introduction:

In this book I will attempted to identify many of the factors that have influenced the culture of the people of present day country of Greece. We will, along the way, explore and learn about the Greek mythical Gods, its many ancient sites of archaeological interest, its history, geography, religion, culture, its special places and finally some of the customs and beliefs of its people. This is in an attempt to answer the question what is it about Greece, its people and its many beautiful Islands that people love so much and inspire them to want to come back to time and time again…

Introduction:

Greece is located in south-eastern Europe, on the southern end of the Balkan Peninsula (Haemus peninsula); it lies at the meeting point of three continents these being Europe, Asia and Africa. Greece has borders to the North with Bulgaria and the Former Yugoslav Republic of Macedonia (F.Y.R.O.M.), to the Northwest with Albania, to the Northeast with Turkey; to the West it is washed by the Ionian Sea; to the South by the Mediterranean Sea and to the East by the Aegean Sea. Mainland Greece is a mountainous land almost completely surrounded by the Mediterranean Sea. Greece has more than 6000 Islands and Islets. The country enjoys mild winters and long, hot and dry summers. The ancient Greeks were a seafaring people. They traded with other countries around the Mediterranean. Many Greek cities created settlements overseas known as colonies. Greek cities were founded around the Black Sea, North Africa, Italy, Sicily, France and Spain. Many tales and legends grew up about Greece. It was seen as a very mysterious land with strange creatures that could be found somewhere across the sea…

Introduction:

The total area of Greece is 131,957 km² and it consists of three main geographical areas. It has a peninsular mainland which extends from the region of Central Greece on the South to the region of Thrace on the North which is the biggest geographic feature of the country. Then there is the Peloponnese peninsula that is separated from the mainland by the canal of the Corinth Isthmus and finally around 6,000 Islands and islets, scattered in the Aegean and Ionian Sea, most of them grouped into clusters that forms the unique Greek archipelago. Crete, Rhodes, Corfu, Skiathos, Kefalonia, Zakynthos, Thassos, the Dodecanese and the Cyclades are just some of the famous and most popular Islands and Island clusters in Greece. Eighty percent of the country consists of mountains or hills, making Greece one of the most mountainous countries of Europe; furthermore, it has 16.000 kilometres of coastline of which 7500 are found around the Islands of the Greek archipelago, a truly unparalleled phenomenon on the European continent. Greece is also famous as the birthplace of modern civilisation …

Introduction:

On the Greek Mainland and Islands customs and traditions are an important aspect of Greek culture. There are either of a religious character or they have their roots in paganism. Most of the old traditions and festivals are still celebrated today. The Greeks are very superstitious and believe in religion but also in supernatural or paranormal phenomenon. Traditions and superstitions vary from Island to Island, from village to village and from region to region. A very important tradition in Greece is that most Greeks are named after a religious saint. It is also the custom in Greece to get engaged before getting married. The man has to ask for the hand of the woman from her father and close family, while the two families give presents to both bride and groom. In Greece, the Carnival is called "Apokries" and is believed to have come from paganism, and more precisely from the old festivities worshiping Dionysus, the god of wine and feast. Easter is the most important festival/celebration for the Greeks, even more so than Christmas. The Greeks are also very superstitious and believe in things such as the evil eye, a black cat being bad luck and there being such things as hobgoblins. Unlike in the western belief, in Greece the unlucky day is Tuesday the 13th and not Friday the 13th. When two Greek people say the same thing together at the same time, they immediately say "piase kokkino" (touch red) one to another and they both have to touch any red item they can find around them. This happens because Greeks believe that saying the same thing is an omen and that the two people will get into a fight or an argument if they don't touch something red. So now that I have introduced Greece, myself and given you a flavour of what the people of Greece believe in, if you are ready, we will start our journey together into the first chapter which is about the many Greek Gods…

The Gods of Greek Mythology

The Ancient Greeks were a very religious people, and they worshiped their Greek Gods and Greek Goddesses with passion. Interestingly the Ancient Greeks believed that their Gods and Goddesses had human qualities alongside magical capabilities. In Greek mythology there were 12 Gods who lived on the summit of Mt. Olympus, which is also the highest mountain in Greece…

The Greek God Zeus

The Gods of Greece

Zeus was the King of the Gods. He and his brothers Hades and Poseidon were in charge of the whole universe. Hades ruled the Underworld, the world of the dead. Poseidon ruled the seas. Zeus, the greatest of the three, ruled the earth and the sky. He controlled the weather, causing wind and rain. He also caused thunder and lightning. He threw his thunderbolt like a spear. Zeus was a good reminder that the gods were not perfect. For one thing, he was not all-powerful. His daughters, the three Fates, decided the futures of both gods and mortals. Zeus couldn't overrule their decisions. And although Zeus was often wise, he could also be foolish. He could also be selfish and even sometimes cruel. He was not a good husband to Hera, the Queen of the Gods. He was not a good father to many of his children. Not surprisingly, the other gods sometimes rebelled against his rule. Most of the gods and mortals respected Zeus. He gave laws and justice to mortals. He taught them kindness and good manners. One story shows how much Zeus prized hospitality and kindness toward strangers. Zeus liked to travel, sometimes in disguise. Once he was travelling with his son Hermes, the messenger god, in a land called Phrygia. They were both disguised as ordinary mortal men. They stopped at all the houses in Phrygia, asking for food and a place to stay the night. Time and time again, they were rudely turned away. Even rich people turned them away. At last they arrived at the home of an elderly couple, a woman named Baucis and a man named Philemon…

The Greek God Zeus

Zeus…

Baucis and Philemon were extremely poor. Even so, they treated the travellers kindly, inviting them into their home for food and drink. They allowed the disguised gods to spend the night. The next day, Hermes and Zeus took off their disguises. Everyone could see that they were gods. Zeus punished the couple's Phrygian neighbours with a terrible flood. All houses were destroyed, except the little hut of Baucis and Philemon. Zeus turned it into a beautiful temple. As a reward for their kindness, Zeus offered the couple anything that they wanted. Because they had lived happily together all their lives, they asked never to be parted. Even in death they wanted to remain together. Baucis and Philemon spent the rest of their lives serving as the temple's priestess and priest. When they died they turned into two trees growing out of the same trunk. In summary: Zeus was the god of the sky and ruler of the Olympian Gods. He overthrew his father, Cronus, and then drew lots with his brothers Poseidon and Hades, in order to decide who would succeed their father on the throne. Zeus won the draw and became the supreme ruler of the gods, as well as lord of the sky and rain. He was married to Hera but often tested her patience, as he was infamous for his many affairs. Zeus was the King of the Gods. He could control the weather. The ancient Greeks believed that when lightning struck earth, it was a sign of Zeus being present. Zeus was also concerned with hospitality. If you treated a guest or stranger badly you could outrage Zeus. His Roman name was Jupiter…

The Greek God Ares

Ares…

Ares was the God of War. He wore body armour and a helmet, and he carried a shield, sword, and spear. He was big and strong and had a fierce war cry, but his war cry was mostly just a lot of noise. Ares did not fight at all well. The armoured Goddess Athena on the other hand was a much better warrior. The Ancient Greeks did not like war, and they did not like Ares, either. They considered him to be a troublemaker. Like many troublemakers, Ares was a coward and a bully. In fact, Ares was never really of any use to anybody in a war. One time a group of giants declared war on the Gods. The giants wanted to rule the entire universe. To keep Ares out of the fighting, they sneaked up on him and knocked him out cold, then they stuffed him into a jar. The other Gods heard Ares screaming for somebody to let him out. They just ignored him because they figured they could fight better without him. They went on to defeat the giants, and then they let Ares out of the jar after the battle was over. Ares bragged about how he could have beaten the giants if he had been set free. The other Gods only laughed. Ares never stayed loyal to one side or the other in a war. He just enjoyed watching people fighting and dying. The war between Greece and Troy was one of the worst ever fought, and even the Gods joined in the battle. When the war started, Ares promised his mother, Hera, to help the Greeks. But he was in love with the goddess Aphrodite, so she easily talked him into helping the Trojans. The Trojans would have been just as happy without Ares's help. Always the bully, he did not pick fights with other Gods. Instead, he challenged a mortal Greek warrior named Diomedes, but Diomedes wounded Ares. Ares liked to cause pain for others, but he whined and complained whenever he got hurt. This time was no different. The wound he got from Diomedes was not very serious, but even so, Ares didn't keep fighting. He went running back to Olympus, the home of the Gods, and wept and wailed to his father Zeus. Even though Zeus bandaged up his wound, he was not at all proud of his warrior son…

The Greek God Eros

Eros   Wine of the Gods

Eros was the Greek God of love, son of Aphrodite and either Ares or Hermes. In some myths, he was considered a primordial God, a child of Chaos, who blessed the union of Gaia and Uranus after which the universe came into existence. In Greek mythology and religion Eros was the God of love. He is more commonly known by his Roman name of Cupid. The Greek myth says that he could infect anyone with love if they were stabbed by one of his arrows.

The Greek God Dionysus

Dionysus was a fun loving God of high spirits, strong emotions and loved wine. He is also closely associated with drama and the theatre. His Roman name was Pluto. Dionysus was the God of grapes and wine. Records of him found on old Mycenaean Greek scripts show us that he was worshipped from 1500 - 1100 BC. He was one of the most jolly Greek Gods however could be wild if opposed. He had many followers who were called Bacchantes who were keen wine drinkers. Dionysus and Demeter were both called the Gods of Harvest…

The Greek God Hades

Hades…

The brothers Zeus, Poseidon, and Hades were the most important Gods of all. Zeus was the strongest and wisest of the three and ruled over the earth. Poseidon ruled the seas. Hades ruled the Underworld, the world of the dead. Hades had dark hair and a dark beard, and he drove a chariot drawn by four dark horses. He was married to Persephone, the queen of the dead. Neither Gods nor mortals liked Hades very much. This was not really fair. Hades wasn't mean or cruel. It just was not his job to be kind or merciful. His duty was to make sure the dead stayed in the Underworld forever. Few mortals ever went to the Underworld and made it back alive. One of these was the great singer Orpheus. When his wife, Eurydice, died, Orpheus went to the Underworld to bring her back. Orpheus's singing delighted Hades, so he agreed to let him take Eurydice back home. Hades made one rule, though. Orpheus wasn't allowed to look at Eurydice as they fled the Underworld. But along the way, Orpheus turned to see if Eurydice was still following him. So she had to stay in the world of the dead forever. There aren't many stories about Hades. Because he rarely left the Underworld, he seldom had any adventures…

The Greek God Hades

Hercules and Cerberus

Hades just went about the unpleasant business of ruling the dead. When he did go out into the world of the living, it usually ended badly for him. Once Hades left his realm in search of Sisyphus, the King of Corinth. Sisyphus was one of the cleverest mortals who ever lived. He managed to cheat death time and time again. Hades planned to put Sisyphus in handcuffs and take him to the Underworld. Instead, the tricky King talked Hades into trying on the handcuffs himself. As long as Sisyphus held Hades hostage, nobody would ever die. The Gods could not allow that, so they pestered Sisyphus into letting Hades loose. Sisyphus himself finally died and went to the Underworld. The Gods knew that he might still be up to mischief even there. So they sentenced him to an impossible task. Sisyphus had to roll a huge boulder up a hill, only to have it roll back down again. Then he had to roll it back up the hill, only to have it roll down yet again. Poor Sisyphus had to do this again and again forever. At least it kept him from causing Hades any more trouble. Eventually, the world of the dead itself came to be called Hades, after its King. A fierce three-headed dog named Cerberus guarded Hades. The river Styx flowed between Hades and the world of the living. A ferryman named Charon rowed dead souls across the Styx. In summary In Greek mythology, Hades the God of the underworld, was a son of the Titans Cronus and Rhea. He had three sisters, Demeter, Hestia, and Hera, as well as two brothers, Zeus, the youngest of the three, and Poseidon. His Roman name was Pluto. Hades was the God of the underworld. Hades had two brothers Zeus and Poseidon and the three of them defeated the Titans, it was this victory that crowned him King of the underworld. Not surprisingly Hades character was fairly depressing despite being very wealthy…

The Greek God Poseidon

Poseidon…

The brothers Zeus, Hades, and Poseidon were the most important Gods of all. Zeus was the strongest and wisest of the three and ruled over the earth. Hades ruled the Underworld, the world of the dead. Poseidon ruled the seas. He was also the God of earthquakes and horses. Poseidon had a beard and long blue hair. He drove a golden cart called a chariot. It was pulled by strange beasts that were half-horse and half-snake. Fish and dolphins always swam along beside the sea God's chariot. Poseidon carried a three-pointed spear called a trident. He used this to start earthquakes or bring water out of the ground. Like the sea he ruled, Poseidon could be either calm or stormy. As you might guess, the God of earthquakes had a short temper. He did not get along with the other Gods. He didn't always get along with mortals, either. The people of Troy once asked Poseidon to help build a wall around their city. He helped, but then he got angry when he did not get paid for his work. He was Troy's enemy ever after that. When Troy fought a terrible war against Greece, Poseidon supported the Greeks. Each God had a city to protect and watch over. The city showed its thanks by honouring that god especially. Maybe because he was ill-tempered, Poseidon had trouble finding a city to honour him. The people of Athens chose Athena instead of Poseidon as its protector. The people of Naxos chose Dionysus…

The Greek God Poseidon

Poseidon…

The people of Aegina chose Zeus. Finally, all the Gods had special cities except Poseidon. He was very unhappy and disappointed. But at long last, the people of Atlantis chose Poseidon. Atlantis was a huge Island, and its people loved and honoured him. There he fell in love with a mortal princess named Clito. He built a palace for her, and they had ten sons. The sons grew up to be Kings who ruled different parts of Atlantis. Those Kings ruled wisely, and Atlantis became the greatest civilisation in the world. Poseidon was proud and happy. But bad times came. The first Kings of Atlantis died, and their sons were bad rulers. And the sons who came after them were worse yet. Years passed, and Atlantis was no longer the world's greatest civilisation. It was actually the worst. It had become both wicked and foolish. Finally, the people of Atlantis forgot to worship Poseidon. The sea God became angry and used his trident to start a terrible earthquake. Atlantis sank beneath the waves, never to be seen again. In summary Poseidon was the God of the sea and horses. He was the brother of Zeus. He was known for his bad temper and was greatly feared because of his ability to cause earthquakes. He was believed to be able to make fresh water gush forth from the earth. His Roman name was Neptune. Poseidon is one of the most famous Greek Gods, and was God of the sea. He was bad tempered and was known to trigger earthquakes and storms whenever he was angry…

The Greek God Apollo

Apollo…

Apollo was the twin brother of Artemis, the Goddess of the hunt and the Moon. Like his sister, Apollo loved hunting with a bow and arrow. He was the God of wisdom, poetry, and music. Apollo was a handsome God, with long black hair. He drove a golden chariot drawn by swans. He was the leader of the Muses, the nine Goddesses of the arts. This God liked lions, wolves, stags, crows, and dolphins. He also liked cattle, and once had a herd of his own. The baby Hermes stole that herd from him. But Apollo let Hermes keep the cattle in return for his lyre. The lyre was a kind of harp that Hermes had made out of a tortoise shell. When Apollo was still a young God, he wanted to know his future. So he went to a town called Delphi, where a priestess was said to tell fortunes. She was called an "oracle." When Apollo arrived in Delphi, he found trouble awaiting him. A monster named Python was supposed to guard the oracle. But Python had turned cruel and was terrorising the people of Delphi. Apollo killed Python with his bare hands. Then the citizens of Delphi built a temple in his honour. The oracle kept telling people's fortunes there. After that, Apollo became known as the God of prophecy—which means the ability to foretell the future…

The Greek God Apollo

Apollo…

The God Apollo was believed to always tell the truth and he was also known as a great healer. However, he sometimes caused diseases as well. His son, Asclepius, was the God of medicine for a while. But Asclepius grew so powerful that he could raise the dead. The Gods could not allow that, so Zeus killed Asclepius with his thunderbolt. Because Apollo was called the God of light, he was sometimes mistaken for the Sun God. The real God of the sun was Helios, who drove a flaming chariot across the sky. Helios once made a terrible mistake. He allowed his half-mortal son Phaeton to drive his chariot. But Phaeton could not control Helios's horses. He almost destroyed the world with that flaming chariot. Like Asclepius, Phaeton was killed by Zeus's thunderbolt. In summary Apollo was the God of the sun, truth, music, poetry, dance and healing. Poets and bards put themselves under his protection. His Roman name was also Apollo. Apollo was the Greek God of light, the sun, music, truth and prophecy, healing. Despite his calm temper and healing nature Apollo had a dark side, where he could bring illness and plague to those that crossed him. Apollo famously drove the sun chariot across the sky with Helios…

The Greek God Uranus

Uranus (meaning "sky" or "heaven") was the primal Greek God personifying the sky. His equivalent in Roman mythology was Caelus. In Ancient Greek literature, Uranus or Father Sky was the son and husband of Gaia, Mother Earth. Uranus was the first Greek God of the sky. Uranus was the son and husband of Gaea. According to some Greek myths Gaea conceived Uranus without a father, yet some records indicate that Aether was his father. Once Uranus was born Gaea chose to marry him bringing together the earth and the sky…

The Greek God Hermes

Hermes…

Hermes was the messenger God. He was young and intelligent-looking. He wore a winged hat and winged sandals, and he carried a magic wand. (We know what he looked like because so many sculptors made statues of him.) Hermes was said to be the God of the marketplace. Oddly, he was also said to be the God of thieves. He himself was a clever thief. He started stealing early in life, actually on the day he was born. His father was Zeus, the King of the Gods. His mother was a young Goddess named Maia. He was born in a mountain cave, and only a few minutes after his birth, Hermes decided to make himself a toy. He picked up a tortoise shell and tied strings across it, then plucked the strings. That was how Hermes invented the first musical instrument, which was called a lyre. And he invented music too! His playing and singing put his mother to sleep. Then, when Hermes was still only an hour or two old, he left the cave and went out to look around at the world. He soon found a herd of cattle that belonged to the God Apollo. The baby Hermes liked the cattle and decided to steal them. When Apollo wasn't looking, Hermes tied branches to the cows' tails. As he led them away, the branches dragged along and erased their hoof prints. Then he hid the cattle and went back to his cave. He climbed back up into his sleeping mother's arms. When she woke up, she had no idea that he'd even been away…

The Greek God Hermes

When Apollo managed to track down Hermes, he was surprised to see that the thief was just a new-born baby. Even so, he demanded his cattle back. Then Hermes started playing the lyre. Apollo was so delighted by the music that he let Hermes keep the cattle in exchange for the lyre. After that, Apollo carried the lyre everywhere and became known as the God of music. Hermes never stopped being full of mischief. But when he grew up, the Gods learned that they could count on him for one important task. With his winged hat and sandals, he ran and flew as fast as the wind, so Zeus named him the messenger of the Gods. Whenever the Gods wanted to send messages to mortals, they gave the job to Hermes. Although he didn't always tell the truth himself, he always delivered those messages just the way he was supposed to. In summary Hermes was the God of travel, business, weights and measures and sports. He was the messenger of the Gods and guided the souls of the dead to the underworld. He was also the patron of herdsmen, thieves, graves and messengers. His staff caused men to fall asleep instantly. His Roman name was Mercury. Hermes was known as the messenger of the Greek Gods. Alongside being a messenger he was the God of travelers, shepherds and merchants. Hermes is famously responsible for passing the dead onto Hades in the underworld…

The Greek God Cronus

Ancient Minoan Knossos on the island of Crete

Kronos (Cronus) was the King of the Titans and the God of time, in particular time when viewed as a destructive, all-devouring force. He ruled the cosmos during the Golden Age after castrating and deposing his father Ouranos (Uranus, Sky). In fear of a prophecy that he would in turn be overthrown by his own son, Kronos swallowed each of his children as they were born. Rhea managed to save the youngest, Zeus, by hiding him away on the Island of Krete (Crete), and fed Kronos a stone wrapped in swaddling clothes. The God grew up, forced Kronos to disgorge his swallowed offspring, and led the Olympians in a ten year war against the Titanes (Titans), driving them in defeat into the pit of Tartaros (Tartarus). Many human generations later, Zeus released Kronos and his brothers from their prison, and made the old Titan King of the Elysian Islands, home of the blessed dead. In summary his Roman name was Saturn Cronus was the King of all the Greek Gods until Zeus took his place. Greek myths indicate that he had an evil side, one myth is that he swallowed all five of his children. He swallowed his children because he feared that they may plan to kill him to get the thrown, ironically he de-thrones his own father by killing him…

The Greek God Hephaestus

Hephaestus…

Hephaestus was the God of fire. He was a blacksmith whose forge was in a volcano. His helpers were one-eyed giants called Cyclopes. He worked in bronze, iron, silver, and gold. He also made things out of clay, including living creatures. From clay he made Pandora, the first mortal woman in the world. Hephaestus made many useful things for the Gods. For the messenger God Hermes, he made a winged hat and winged sandals. For the sun God Helios, he made a golden chariot to ride across the sky. For Eros, the God of love, he made a silver bow with silver arrows. Hephaestus was a good-natured God who usually got along well with everybody. Even so, his mother, Hera, once got angry with him. She threw him off Olympus, the mountain where the Gods lived. When he hit the ground, he broke his foot. A Goddess named Thetis nursed him back to health. But he walked with a limp after that. Good natured though he was, Hephaestus did not forgive Hera. And he finally got even with her. He made a beautiful throne out of gold and offered it to her as a gift. When she sat on it, invisible chains wrapped around her wrists. She couldn't get out of the throne, which rose up into the air. All the Gods tried to talk Hephaestus into letting Hera loose. Hephaestus finally did release Hera when the beautiful Goddess Aphrodite agreed to marry him…

The Greek God Hephaestus

Hephaestus and Aphrodite was not a happy marriage, though. Aphrodite was really in love with Ares, the God of war. The Goddess Thetis had a half-mortal son named Achilles. When Achilles was a baby, she bathed him in the river Styx. This was supposed to make him invulnerable, meaning impossible to hurt or kill. Even so, Thetis worried when Achilles got ready to go fight in the Trojan War. Hephaestus made the best weapons and armour in the world. So Thetis asked Hephaestus to make a shield and armour for Achilles. Hephaestus was still grateful to Thetis for helping him after his fall from Olympus. So he was happy to do as she asked. Hephaestus's armour did not let Achilles down during the war. But Thetis had made one mistake. When she had dipped Achilles in the river Styx, she had held him by the heel. So his heel was not invulnerable. Achilles was killed by an arrow in his heel. In summary Hephaestus was the God of fire, volcanoes, blacksmiths and craft-workers. He was lame and this led to him being thrown out of Mount Olympus. He was married to the Goddess Aphrodite. He was the father of Erechtheus the legendary King of Athens. His Roman name was Vulcan. Hephaestus was the Greek God of blacksmiths, craftsmen, sculptors, and fire. Hephaestus was the son of Zeus and Hera…

The Greek Goddess Athena

Athena…

Athena was tall, strong, graceful, grey-eyed, and she liked owls. From the beginning, she was a pretty amazing Goddess. In fact, even her birth was most unusual. Zeus, the father of Gods and Goddesses, was also Athena's father. Her mother was a mortal woman named Metis. Older Gods had warned Zeus that he would be in trouble if Metis gave birth to a daughter. So he swallowed Metis whole. When it came time for Athena to be born, she sprang full grown out of Zeus's head. She was completely dressed in armour, as she always would be. She also carried a shield and a spear. As you might guess about a woman in armour, she was a great warrior. Athena was also a Goddess of wisdom. She taught people about arts and crafts. She also taught them how to think clearly and live well. She was often seen with an owl, so owls became a symbol of wisdom. Athena didn't get along with the sea God Poseidon. For one thing, they were often rivals over one thing or another. Once the people of a new city were looking for a God to watch over and protect them. Athena and Poseidon both wanted the job. To impress the city's citizens, the two Gods gave them gifts. Poseidon struck the ground with his three-pointed spear, and water poured out. The water turned into a river that flowed into the sea. Poseidon told the people to build ships to sail to the sea. He said that they could travel everywhere. They could become the most powerful people on earth. The citizens were indeed impressed. But then Athena told them to taste the water…

The Greek Goddess Athena

Athena…

The water tasted awful. It was saltwater, which is impossible to drink. Then Athena gave the citizens her gift. When she hit the ground with her spear, a tree magically grew up within seconds. She explained that it was a special tree. It was an olive tree. Its wood was good both for building houses and for heating those houses in winter. Better still, the tree's little green fruits, called "olives," were delicious. And oil made out of the olives was useful for cooking. The citizens liked Athena's gift better than Poseidon's. Not only did they choose Athena to watch over them, they named the city after her. They called it Athens. Poseidon left in a huff, causing a serious flood on his way. But the Athenians were not bothered very much. With Athena's help, their city grew to be strong and wealthy. Athens became one of the greatest cities of all time. Today it's the capital and the largest city of Greece. In summary Athena is the Goddess of war and cunning wisdom. She is also the Goddess of pot-making and wool-working. She is associated with the city, and almost every town in Greece had a sanctuary dedicated to Athena. She invented the chariot, the bridle and built the first ship. The olive tree is sacred to her. Her Roman name was Minerva. Her parents were Zeus and Metis and her sibling was Porus. In Greek mythology and religion Athena was the Goddess of wisdom, strategy, mathematics, law and justice, and crafts and skill. Athena always tried to avoid conflict however when she needed to fight Athena always won…

The Greek Goddess Nike

In ancient Greek religion Nike was a Goddess who personified victory, also known as the Winged Goddess of Victory. The Roman equivalent was Victoria. Some Greek myths describe Nike as the daughter of Pallas and the sister of Kratos, Bia and Zelus. The Greek word 'Nike' is often translated to 'victory', and there is a certain trainer manufacturer named after her.

The Greek Goddess Hera

Hera…

Hera was the Queen of the Gods and the protector of women. Her husband Zeus ruled the earth and sky. She was the mother of the war God Ares and the forge God Hephaestus. Her daughter, Ilithyia, was the Goddess of childbirth. Hera was beautiful and graceful. But she was also stern and bossy. And she could be very vain about her good looks. Hera was furious when she lost a beauty contest with Athena and Aphrodite. Another time, a mortal queen claimed to be more beautiful than Hera. The Goddess turned that queen into a crane. Although Hera was the Goddess of marriage, her own marriage was not happy. For one thing, Zeus was always interested in other women. Hera had good reason to be jealous…

The Greek Goddess Hera

Hera…

Once Hera sent a hundred-eyed monster named Argos to spy on Zeus. Even Zeus couldn't get away with much with Argos watching him! Annoyed, Zeus called upon his son Hermes, the messenger God. He ordered Hermes to kill Argos. This was hard to do, because some of Argos's eyes were always awake and watching. But Hermes managed to put all those eyes to sleep. Then he killed Argos as Zeus had commanded. Hera put Argos's eyes in the peacock's tail. The peacock was her favourite bird from that time on. Hera was also fond of cows, lions, and cuckoos. Next, Zeus asked a young Goddess named Echo for help. Echo was a wonderful storyteller. At Zeus's orders, Echo told Hera stories. That kept Hera's attention for hours and hours. Meanwhile, Zeus could sneak away and do whatever he wanted. Hera figured out what was going on. She got very angry with Echo. This was not fair, of course. Echo could not help what she was doing. After all, she couldn't very well disobey the King of the Gods. But when Hera was angry, she could be most unfair. Hera cursed Echo. She took away Echo's power to tell stories. She even took away Echo's power to speak normally. Instead, Echo could only repeat things said by others. Echo became so sad that she disappeared completely. But it is said that you can still hear her voice. If you shout in a canyon or valley, Echo might repeat your words. In summary Hera was the wife of Zeus and the Queen of the Gods. She is the Goddess of weddings and marriage. She was extremely jealous of the many affairs of her husband Zeus. She took terrible revenge on the girlfriends and illegitimate children of her husband. Her Roman name was Juno. Hera was the Queen of the Gods. Hera was the Goddess of women and marriage and was one of Zeus's seven wives…

The Greek Goddess Aphrodite

Aphrodite…

Aphrodite had an unusual birth. She rose up out of sea foam, beautiful and fully grown-up. She was the Goddess of love, and she liked doves, sparrows, and swans. She was married to Hephaestus, the God of the forge, but not at all happily. She was really in love with Ares, the God of war. Aphrodite and her son Eros were in charge of making people and Gods fall in love. Eros used his magic bow and arrow to make that happen. Oddly, this Goddess of love helped start a terrible war. But she didn't really mean to. Eris, the Goddess of discord, liked to stir up trouble. So one day Eris made a golden apple. She wrote the words "For the Fairest" on it. Then she threw this apple where the Goddesses Athena, Hera, and Aphrodite would find it. Each one of them thought she was "the Fairest"and the most beautiful Goddess of them all…

The Greek Goddess Aphrodite

The lady of the water nymphs

The three Goddesses decided to hold a beauty contest. To judge the contest, they chose a mortal named Paris. He was a handsome Prince of Troy. Each Goddess took Paris aside and offered him a gift. If Paris chose Hera, she promised to make him ruler of the world. If he chose Athena, she promised to make him a victorious soldier. But Paris wasn't very ambitious or brave. He was therefore, not interested in either of those offers. Then Aphrodite promised Paris the love of the most beautiful woman in the world. This appealed to Paris much more than the other offers did. So he judged Aphrodite "the Fairest" of the Goddesses, and she got to keep the apple. This was exactly what the trouble making Eris had hoped for. The most beautiful woman in the world happened to be married already. Her name was Helen. She was the Queen of Sparta and the wife of King Menelaus. When Helen and Paris ran away to Troy together, Menelaus was furious. He called all the great warriors of Greece together, and they declared war on Troy. Many thousands of warriors died in the Trojan War, which lasted ten years. It ended with the destruction of Troy. In summary Aphrodite is the Goddess of love and beauty. She was the wife of Hephaistos but was in love with the war God Ares. Her Roman name was Venus. Aphrodite was the Greek Goddess of love and beauty. Zeus was worried about the rivalry and competition between the male Gods who wanted to be with Aphrodite, so he married her to Hephaestus. Aphrodite was very jealous and those who said they were more beautiful than her would feel her anger…

The Greek Goddess Hestia

Hestia…

The beautiful Hestia was the oldest of the Gods of Olympus. She disliked gossip, so hardly any stories were told about her. But it would be a mistake to think she was not important. In some ways, she was the most important of all the Gods. From the earliest times, the other Gods of Olympus all had duties. Hermes carried messages, Ares was in charge of war, Artemis watched over all hunters, and Zeus ruled over everybody. Other Gods had other jobs. But for a time, no one seemed to know what Hestia was supposed to do. One day the Gods Poseidon and Apollo told Zeus that they both loved Hestia. Both of them wanted to marry her. They demanded that Zeus choose between them. Otherwise, war would break out among the Gods. Such a war would have been terrible indeed. But Hestia solved the whole problem very simply. She refused ever to have a husband. Zeus was relieved and grateful to avoid a war. As a reward, he gave Hestia the keys to Olympus. He put her in charge of the Gods everyday business. Hestia made sure that the Gods always had plenty of food, clothing, and money. After all, even Gods have to worry about such things! Zeus also made Hestia the Goddess of homes everywhere…

The Greek Goddess Hestia

Hestia also taught mortals how to build houses. Every Greek house had a sacred spot for her. That was the hearth, the centre of family life. Mortals prayed to Hestia more than to any of the other Gods. Every family meal began and ended with a prayer to Hestia. Whenever a baby was born, the parents carried it around the hearth and prayed to Hestia. Mortals had a saying: "Begin with Hestia." In other words, when doing anything, always start out in the right way. Hestia lived a quiet life, leaving fame and adventure to others. Zeus's half-mortal son Dionysus showed up on Olympus one day. He wanted to have a throne like the other important Gods. Hestia gladly gave up her own throne for him. After all, she was too busy to spend much time sitting there. In summary in Ancient Greek religion, Hestia which means in ancient Greek: "hearth" or "fireside" is a virgin Goddess of the hearth, architecture, and the right ordering of domesticity, the family, and the state. In Greek mythology, she is a daughter of Cronus and Rhea and the eldest of the Olympian Gods. Her Roman name was Vesta. Hestia was the Goddess of the hearth and Greek families worshipped her by their firesides…

The Greek Goddess Gaea (Gaia)

Gaia (Gaea) Goddess of the Earth

Gaia (Gaea) was the Goddess of the earth. She was one of the primordial elemental deities (*protogenoi*) born at the dawn of creation. Gaia was the great mother of all creation and the heavenly Gods were descended from her through her union with Ouranos (Uranus) (Sky), the Sea-Gods from her union with Pontos (Sea), the Gigantes (Giants) from her mating with Tartaros (the Pit), and mortal creatures born directly from her earthy flesh. In summary her Roman name was Terra (which translates to Earth in English). Gaea is the Greek Goddess of earth. She was the second living thing in the universe, the first being the Greek God Chaos. Gaea was the mother of all the Greek Gods. The Titans and Giants descended from her relationship with Uranus (the sky), and the Sea Gods descended from her union with Pontus (the sea)…

The Greek Goddess Psyche

Psykhe (Psyche) was the Goddess of the soul and the wife of Eros (Roman Cupid) God of love. She was once a mortal princess whose extraordinary beauty earned the ire of Aphrodite (Roman Venus) when men began turning their worship away from the Goddess towards the girl. Her Roman name was Psyche and her husband was Eros (Cupid). Psyche is the Goddess of love. The word psyche is the Ancient Greek word for soul or living. She famously courted Cupid (the God of love) for a very long time.

The Greek Goddess Demeter

Demeter was the Goddess of fertility and agriculture. She was an important Goddess for farmers and women. Demeter was also associated with the underworld. Her Roman name was Ceres. Her parents were Cronus and Rhea. Her childs name was Persephone. In Greek mythology and religion Demeter was the Goddess of the harvest. She was responsible for the all of the plants on earth and is linked with fertility. Demeter also controlled the seasons…

Ancient Greek History

Ancient Greek Hero Alexandra the Great

The history of ancient Greece dates back to the stone age, more specifically between the archaic periods of the 8th to 6th centuries BC. The first ancient Greeks were very skilled hunters. Greek hunters are depicted on the famous orange and black illustrations used on ancient Greek vases. The timeline of ancient Greece is as follows: Neolithic: 6000 to 2900 BC - Early Bronze Age: 2900 to 2000 BC - Minoan: 2000 to 1400 BC - Mycenaean: 1600 to 1100 BC - The Dark Age: 1100 to 750 BC - Archaic: 750 to 500 BC - Classical: 500 to 336 BC - Hellenistic: 336 to 146 BC.

The Neolithic Period in Greece (6000 to 2900 BC)

The Neolithic period lasted from 6000 to 2900 BC. Ancient Greek settlements have been found on the mainland of Greece. Archaeological findings indicate that the ancient Greeks in the Neolithic period were the ones that laid the foundations for the cultures and society for the generations of Greek people that followed. The Neolithic Greek people were some of the earliest farmers in the world. Methodical farming, stock rearing, bartering and pottery steadied the economy of the region. People formed settlements in Greece, rather than moving from place to place. Permanent settlements allowed for animals, such as sheep and goats to be domesticated and for the growing of crops…

Ancient Greek History

The Minoans…

The Early Bronze Age in Greece (2900 to 2000 BC)

In the ancient Greek Bronze Age, which lasted approximately 3000 years, the people of Greece developed significant advances in technical, economic and social improvements. At this time, the ancient Greeks were more developed than its neighbouring countries. This meant that Greece was at the centre of civilisation and culture in the Mediterranean.

The Minoan and Mycenaean Period in Greece (2000 to 1100 BC)

The Mycenaean and Minoan civilisation followed the early Bronze Age in Greece. It arose during the Bronze Age period of Greek history. The Mycenaean and Minoan were farmers who lived of the land and produced grain, olives and grapes that they used to make wine. The Mycenaean society was ruled by a warrior aristocracy. The Minoans society advanced through trade, whereas the Mycenaeans benefited from conquest.

The Dark Age in Greece (1100 to 750 BC)

Archaeological evidence shows that the birth of the Dark Age in Greece followed the end of the Bronze Age. The Dark Age is known for its wars and invasions which meant that the Greek civilisation had to adapt quickly. The majority of Mycenaean palaces and settlements were either destroyed or abandoned, with the exception of the one in Athens. The population of Ancient Greece fell dramatically at this time and people lived in small settlements/groups. These groups of people lived off the crops they grew and the animals they reared. Moving frequently to find suitable areas of grazing for their pastoral and livestock needs. The Dark Age came to an end in 750 BC…

Ancient Greek History

The Greek God Athena…

The Archaic Period in Greece (750 to 500 BC)

The Archaic period in Greece was a happier era than the Dark Age which preceded it. This more settled time led to enhancements in politics during which the theories of democracy were begun. Culture and art improved too and much of the art seen in the Archaic Period is said to have influenced artists in the Classical period which followed. Literacy and the knowledge of writing was re-established in Greece. These skills had been lost throughout the Dark Ages.

The Classical Period in Greece (500 to 336 BC)

This was, as the name suggests, a time when Greece enjoyed an explosion of drama, the arts and learning. In the Classical Period the famous Ancient Greek King called Alexander the Great lived and died in 323 BC. His death is surrounded in mystery as supposedly he died from a mysterious illness. It is thought that he had a relapse of malaria or caught an illness at a drinking party. During the classical period the Greeks came into conflict with the Kingdom of Persia, to the east of Greece. Politics had progressed and a democratic government was introduced under the leadership of the Athenian statesman called Pericles.

The Hellenistic Period in Greece (336 to 146 BC)

The Hellenistic age marked a turning point for ancient Greek civilisation. The society changed from a localised and introverted culture to an open and cosmopolitan one, meaning that the Greeks embraced the practices of many different countries and cultures…

Ancient Greek History

The Ancient Greek Olympics started in 776 BC

The Ancient Greeks pioneered sporting contests and one of those contests was the Olympic Games. Records indicate that the first Olympic Games began in 776 BC at Olympia in the southwest of mainland Greece. The Ancient Greek Olympics were very popular and took place every four years. They were held in honour of the Greek God Zeus. Interestingly women were not allowed to compete and only Greek national men were allowed to enter the competition. Initially the Olympic Games begun as a one day contest of wrestling and athletics, however the games quickly developed to last a week and have many more sports. An often forgotten fact was that there were other sporting contests alongside the Olympic Games such as the; Pythian Games which took place every four years just outside of Delphi. And the Isthmos Games which took place every two years near Corinth. Although both were very popular neither of them could compete with the Greek Olympics. According to Greek mythology the God Heracles was the founder of the Ancient Greek Olympics. Some records indicate that Heracles ran a race in Olympia and declared that the race should be repeated every four years. Winners were presented with a wreath of laurel leaves, which were highly regarded by the Ancient Greeks, due to the God Apollo being known for wearing a laurel wreath. When the modern day Olympics were revived the laurel was appropriately chosen to symbolise the games…

Ancient Greek History

The Ancient Greek Olympics

The first ever winner of the Greek Olympics was a baker from the region of Eleia which was the region of Olympia where the Olympic Games were founded. He was called Coroebus. To celebrate the Games a Statue of Zeus which was made of gold and ivory was placed inside the temple at Olympia. It was 42 feet tall and was one the ancient Seven Wonders of the World. Although women were not allowed to compete in the Ancient Greek Olympics there was one instance where this was not the case, and she actually won!

Did you know?

In 396 BC a daughter of a Spartan King called Kyniska won the four horse chariot race known as the tethrippon. She found a loophole in the regulations which allowed women to compete as horse owners (not in the actual race).

Women who were married were given the death penalty if they watched an Olympic event.

Should a competitor back out of an event he was fined for cowardice.

The primary stadium where the ancient Greek Olympics were held could hold 45,000 spectators. It was located on the archaeological site of Olympia.

Spectators travelled from every region of Greece and stayed in tents pitched around the stadium.

The first ever event of the Ancient Greek Olympics was a foot race of 190 meters.

If a race was tied then the race had to be re-run. Unlike with modern day Olympic runners ancient Greek athletes started the race standing up…

Ancient Greek History

The Ancient Greek Olympics

A Greek poet called Pausanias wrote stories about how the athletes trained and performed in their races. He tells us that "the ancient Greek athletes were naked when competing". Competing naked promoted the appreciation of the male body and was also a homage to the Gods. Interestingly the word gymnasium which derives from the Greek word gymnos means naked. Ancient Greece was a turbulent place to live in during this time and wars and disputes were common. To protect athletes when travelling to Olympic events a truce, called the Olympic truce, was made where wars and disputes were halted for the duration of the Olympic Games. Each Greek state was represented by an athlete or team of athletes. In modern day Olympics it is whole countries that compete with one another. One of the events that took place in the ancient Greek Olympics was the Hoplitodromos. Competitors would run either 365 or 731 meters wearing a full suit of armour. This would have been rather comical for spectators as competitors often tripped, collided and/or fell short of the finish line. On the final day of the ancient Greek Olympics 100 oxen were sacrificed to the Gods and all the competitors gathered for a huge feast. It is widely believed that the ancient Greek Olympics were stopped by the Roman emperor Theodosius (or his grandson) in either 393 AD or 435 AD…

The Ancient Sites of Greece

A Minoan Fisherman…

Ancient Greece was the cradle of democracy. It is the civilisation which produced some of the most ground breaking art, philosophy and culture the world has ever seen, the Ancient Greeks left their legacy in a myriad of ways. Many of the Ancient Greek sites and ruins that have survived today are among the most famous landmarks in the world. The Acropolis in Athens stands tall as a testament to Ancient Greek achievement. Yet there is a multitude of Ancient Greek sites and Ancient Greek places that are still able to be seen today, some equally as famous, others less so. In the following pages we will visit a selection of some of the best Ancient sites and ruins in Greece…

The Ancient Sites of Greece

The Acropolis of Athens

The Acropolis is one of the most recognisable historic sites in the world and remains an inspirational monument to the achievements of the Ancient Greek civilisation. Standing tall above the Greek City of Athens, the Acropolis contains a number of important buildings and monuments from Greek Antiquity, including the Parthenon, the Erechtheion and the Propylaiaand the temple of Athena Nike. The majority of the sites on the Acropolis were constructed in the 5th Century BC, during the 'golden age' of Athens and under the stewardship of Athenian statesman Pericles. After the original site was burned to the ground in 480 BC during the Persian Wars, the Athenians set to re-building their city with monuments that would bear testament to the greatness of their state. The Acropolis continued to be developed throughout the Hellenistic, Macedonian and Roman periods. After these eras came the Christian era and the Acropolis complex was largely converted for use as a Christian centre, with the Parthenon serving as a Cathedral. However, by the early middle ages, the Acropolis was more frequently used as a defensive fortification by the various occupiers of the city. During a battle between Venetian and Ottoman forces in 1687, the Parthenon suffered severe damage which was never repaired. These impressive monuments have largely stood the test of time through invasion, conquest and war and the Acropolis stands as one of the greatest historic destinations in the world. Today, the Acropolis is an extremely popular historic site and caters for a multitude of tourists every year. I have been there and it is truly an utterly inspiring place…

The Ancient Sites of Greece

Olympia

In ancient times Olympia was a vibrant Ancient Greek City. It is believed that the site of Olympia was inhabited from 3000 BC, however it was after the fall of the Mycenaean civilisation that the city began to flourish and, by 900 BC it was already considered an important religious site. The Olympic Games of 776 BC, the first Olympic Games, were held in the city in honour of the Greek deity, Zeus. The games at Olympia were a national event and attracted participants and spectators from all around the country, raising the status of Olympia. The games would continue until 394 AD when Roman Emperor Theodosius I, seeing them as a "pagan cult", ended them. Even so Olympia began to develop and grow. Today the result of this gradual growth can be seen at Olympia through sites such as the Treasuries, the Temple of Hera, both of religious importance and contained in the sacred precinct known as the Altis and the Pelopion, the supposed tomb of the mythical Pelops. These were built in around 600 BC. Even the stadium in which the Olympic Games were played was upgraded, a purpose built area being built in around 560 BC which was able to seat approximately 50,000 people. The remains of this impressive stadium are still visible today…

The Ancient Sites of Greece

Epidaurus

Epidaurus was a major city in Ancient Greece and was famed as a centre for healing. It was inhabited since prehistoric times, Epidaurus thrived as a sanctuary devoted to the healing deities including Apollo, Asklepios and Hygeia and contained hundreds of spas, the remains of many of which can still be seen today. The main sanctuary area, called the Asklepieion, contains two such spas where a variety of healing rituals took place in ancient times, including hypnosis. There is also a shrine to Asklepios and the remains of rooms for the treating of visiting patients. The most impressive of the sites at Epidaurus is the fourth century BC theatre, which was built to accommodate approximately 15,000 people and is still extremely well preserved. Whilst most of the sites at Epidaurus were constructed in the fourth and fifth centuries BC, when the city was at its peak, some of them date back as far as the Mycenaean period and others were also adapted later by the Romans. The theatre is one example of such refurbishments. Epidaurus is an absolutely vast, fascinating site set over three levels and offering an insight into Ancient Greek life. I can still remember the day that I visited the site and the feeling of excitement and wonder that I felt standing there on the stage of the theatre and seeing all those sets of terraced seats laid out before me…

The Ancient Sites of Greece

Delphi

Delphi is an archaeological site on mainland Greece comprising of well-preserved ruins of one of the most important cities in Ancient Greece. Archaeologists have found evidence that Delphi was inhabited as early as the Neolithic period and has sites dating back to the Mycenaean Civilisation, but it was the Ancient Greek city which developed in Delphi which has left the biggest mark on the area. Many of the sites at Delphi date back to the fifth century BC, although many have been reconstructed and some altered by the Romans. Many of the buildings also suffered from damage and destruction caused by fires and earthquakes. Nevertheless, as I walked through Delphi I found that it offers a fascinating insight into the lives of its former inhabitants even today. Delphi was such an important city and had mythological and religious status. Ancient Greek mythology states that when the deity Zeus released two eagles to find the centre of the world, they met in Delphi. The name "Delphi" derives from the word "dolphin" as it was believed that this was where Apollo arrived on the back of a dolphin. Today, Delphi reveals much of its past through incredible ruins, demonstrating a balance between religion, politics and leisure activities, particularly sports. Amongst these are the Temple of Apollo, believed to date back to the fourth century BC and once a central ceremonial site. Sporting sites, such as the Delphi gymnasium and the stadium are also visible and are very well preserved. Possibly the best preserved site in Delphi is the fifth century Doric building of the Treasury of the Athenians, which is located along The Sacred Way. Perhaps Delphi's most iconic site is the Tholos. Constructed in around 380 BC, this once circular building had six Doric columns, three of which are still standing today…

The Ancient Sites of Greece

Sparta

Sparta was one of the most famous city-states of the ancient world and left not only a mark in our historic records, but its very culture is at the heart of modern language. The English word 'Spartan' is a reflection on their very way of life which was simple, basic and severe. Rising to power in the late 7th Century BC, Sparta produced the most powerful land-army of the Hellenic world. Spartan soldiers led the Greek coalition during the Greco-Persian War, becoming legendary in their heroic last stand at Thermopylae which led to the eventual victory of the Greeks at Plataea. Sparta's star continued to rise in the following century, with victory over Athens in the long-running Peloponnesian War and a brief spell of rule over all of Greece and even parts of Asia Minor. However, it was their constant military involvements combined with their elitist, purist approach to citizenry which led to their downfall. Sparta's conflict with a resurgent Thebes, particularly their defeat at the Battle of Leuctra, crippled Spartan power, a blow from which they never recovered. Their own discriminatory nature left Sparta without the capacity to suffer losses, and therefore one or two severe defeats crippled Sparta's military manpower. Sparta did live on as an independent power for the next two centuries, but the city never wielded real power again. Sparta had no part in the conquests of Alexander the Great, and the city was eventually conquered, along with the rest of Greece, by the Romans in the mid-second century BC. Today, the ruins of ancient Sparta can be found on the outskirts of the modern day city of Sparti…

The Ancient Sites of Greece

The Acropolis of Rhodes

The Acropolis of Rhodes is the site of the main ancient remains of what was once the city of Rhodes in the Hellenistic period. Containing several different sites, including temples, monuments and public buildings, the Acropolis of Rhodes dating to mostly the third and second centuries BC. On the Acropolis of Rhodes, there are some impressively reconstructed sites such as the Odeon and Theatre as well as the ruins of the Temple of Apollo…

The Ancient Sites of Greece

Aigai in Macedonia, Northern Greece

Aigai in northern Greece was once the capital of the Macedonian Kingdom and it was here in 336 BC that Alexander the Great was proclaimed King of Macedon after the assassination of his father, Philip II. Evidence of human occupation on the site stretches back to the 3rd millennium BC, it is thought that it was not until around 1000 BC – 700 BC that it became an important regional centre. Aigai probably reached its height around 500 BC as the Macedonian capital, before being replaced by Pella around 100 years later. After the death of Alexander, Aigai suffered during the Wars of Alexander's Successors and the city was again damaged during the Roman conquest of the region in 168 BC. Aigai survived well into the Roman era but gradually declined during the latter Imperial period. Today, Aigai can be found near the modern town of Vergina and there are a number of interesting sites to explore. Probably the most famous of these sites are the royal burial tombs, which are believed to house the tombs of Phillip II and Alexander the Great's son, Alexander IV. An impressive museum was built to enclose these tombs and visitors can now explore this underground tomb complex. Along with these main tombs there are as many as 300 other grave mounds, some dating back to the 11th century BC in the surrounding area. Other important remains at Aigai include the royal palace which has an impressive mosaics and the 4th century BC theatre, believed to be the exact site of Philip's murder. There are also a number of temples near the theatre, including the temple of Eukleia…

The Ancient Sites of Greece

Amathus on the island of Cyprus

Amathus is an archaeological site in Cyprus containing the remains of one of the Island's oldest ancient towns. Known to have been inhabited since at least 1050 BC, the origins of Amathus are unclear. It is believed to have been founded by the Eteocyprians and to have flourished and grown. Over time, it played host to the Greeks, the Phoenicians, the Persians, the Ptolemies and the Romans. The abandonment of Amathus appears to have occurred in the late seventh century AD. Amathus is strongly connected with the cult of Aphrodite as well as having links to the legend of Ariadne. Today, the ruins of Amathus include several ancient sites, including several tombs, an acropolis with a first century AD Roman temple to Aphrodite, an agora with some public baths and the remains of the eighth century BC palace of Amathus…

The Ancient Sites of Greece

The Ancient Agora of Athens

The Ancient Agora of Athens

The Ancient Agora of Athens was a market, a meeting place and the social, political and commercial hub of the ancient city. Whilst initially developed in the sixth century BC, the Ancient Agora of Athens was destroyed, rebuilt and renovated several times. These were done after attacks by the Persians in 480 BC, the Romans and by the Scandinavian tribe known as the Herulians in 267 BC. Despite its turbulent history, the Ancient Agora of Athens houses several fascinating sites, including the stunning fifth century BC Temple of Hephaestus. It is also home to the remains of several covered walkways or "stoas" such as the famous Stoa of Zeus where Socrates is said to have debated and met with other philosophers. A good way to get your bearings within the Ancient Agora of Athens is to start by visiting the Agora Museum, which offers more information about the whole site…

The Ancient Sites of Greece

Minoan wall paintings

Aptera on the Island of Crete

The archaeological site of Aptera contains an array of interesting Greco-Roman ruins, the highlight of which is probably the remains of the Roman cisterns which originally supplied water to the city's baths. Founded around the 7th century BC, Aptera became one of the most important cities of western Crete and grew into a thriving centre for much of the Hellenic and Roman periods. The city continued to be inhabited into the Byzantine age before a combination of natural disaster and external attacks forced its abandonment, which is dated to 823 AD. Today as well as the impressive Roman cisterns, visitors to Aptera can explore a number of fascinating ruins at the site including Roman baths, villas and an ancient theatre. The archaeological site also includes a small ancient temple most likely dedicated to the goddess Demeter as well as the ruins of several early churches. Also a World War 2 German machine gun post can also be viewed nearby along with a 19th century Turkish castle…

The Ancient Sites of Greece

Asklepieion on the Island of Kos

Asklepieion, also known as Asclepeion, on the Island of Kos was an ancient Greek and Roman sacred centre of healing based on the teachings of Hippocrates. There has been a healing sanctuary at the site of Asklepieion since prehistory, but the main ruins today are those of later sanctuaries. The most significant was dedicated to Asklepios, who was a Greek deity of health. Over time, Asklepieion became increasingly popular and visitors would travels from far and wide to experience its healing properties. Thus, the sanctuary was expanded several times. Today, the pretty and relatively well-preserved ruins of Asklepieion are set over three levels and include several temples, some Roman baths, gateways and a banqueting hall. It is worth noting that this is not the most easily accessible site for people with mobility issues. The terrain is quite steep with many stairs to climb…

The Ancient Sites of Greece

Corinth in the Peloponnese Region of Greece

Ancient Corinth, the ruins of which can be found in the modern town of Korinthos, was a city of major importance in Ancient Greece and in Roman times. Located between mainland Greece and the Peloponnese region, Corinth was a vital port and a thriving city-state as well as being of religious significance. Inhabited since the Neolithic period, Corinth grew from the eight century BC under the Ancient Greeks, developing into a centre of trade and was a city of great riches. Much of this wealth was accumulated from the seventh century BC under the rule of Periander, who exploited Corinth's location on the Isthmus of Corinth. By travelling through Corinth, ships could cross quickly between the Gulf of Corinth and the Saronic Gulf, avoiding the need to sail around the coast. Corinth had the diolkos, a ship hauling device which allowed them to do just that. Ship owners were charged for using this device, providing Corinth with an ongoing flow of income. Corinth became such a powerful city-state that it even established various colonies such as at Syracuse and Epidamnus. In 338 BC, following the Peloponnesian War and the subsequent Corinthian War, Corinth was conquered by Philip II of Macedon. Throughout the classical era, Corinth had held regular sporting tournaments known as the Isthmian Games. These were continued under the Macedonians and, in fact, it was at the 336 BC Isthmus Games that Alexander the Great was selected to lead the Macedonians in the war against Persia…

The Ancient Sites of Greece

Corinth Canal linking Central Greece to the Peloponnese Region

In 146 BC, Corinth suffered partial destruction from the invasion of the Roman general Mummius, although it was later rebuilt under Julius Caesar, eventually growing into an even more prosperous Roman city. Corinth's decline began in 267 AD following the invasion of the Herulians. Over the subsequent years, it would fall into the hands of the Turks, the Knights of Malta, the Venetians and finally the Greeks, each of these conflicts, together with numerous natural disasters, depleting but never entirely destroying the city's once magnificent sites. Another interesting aspect of Corinth is its diverse religious history. Dedicated to the Greek deities of Apollo, Octavia and Aphrodite, during Roman times it was also the home of a large Jewish community as well as being visited by the Apostle Paul. Today, visitors to Corinth can see its many ancient sites, including the fairly well-preserved ruins of the Temple of Apollo, which was built in 550 BC and the remaining columns of the Temple of Octavia. By contrast, only few remnants remain of the former Temple of Aphrodite, once a home of Corinth's sacred prostitutes. Perhaps what makes Corinth such a fascinating site is that, due to its extensive wealth over the years, this ancient city's Doric architecture was exceptionally ornate. Beyond these sacred sites, much of Corinth's original infrastructure is visible along with many remains from the Roman-era city, including the Theatre and the Peirene Fountain…

The Ancient Sites of Greece

The Greek Island of Delos

Delos is an Island and archaeological site which was held sacred by the ancient Greeks as the birthplace of the deity Apollo. It is unclear as to whether his twin sister Artemis was also believed to have been born there. There were temples built in honour of Artemis at Delos, but the legend seems mainly focused on Apollo. Evidence shows that Delos was inhabited as early as the third millennium BC and, from around the tenth century BC, when it was invaded by the Ionian Greeks, it developed into a religious centre as well as a thriving port. It became a site of pilgrimage for many civilisations, Delos was later ruled by the Athenians, under which the native Delians suffered greatly, being exiled on several occasions. Delos was considered such a sacred site that it was forbidden to die or to give birth there. Athenian leader Peisistratus is said to have even rid the island of all of its existing graves in the sixth century BC. Later, severely ill people and pregnant women would be removed from the Island and taken to nearby Rheneia. Over the centuries, activity at Delos centred on the shrines and temples to Apollo in an area known as the Sanctuary of Apollo. Few of the once many temples in the Sanctuary of Apollo remain intact today, but what there is have been beautifully preserved and/or reconstructed. Mosaic floors and statues are dotted around Delos as are the facades of former temples, such as that of the one dedicated to Isis. Some of its most famous statues on the Island are those of the Terrace of the Lions. The originals of these are now kept in the Delos Archaeological Museum, but the on-site replicas do give an idea of how it once would have looked. There is also an ancient theatre on the Island…

The Ancient Sites of Greece

Ancient mosaics in the Greek City of Zeugma

Eleusis on the Plain of Thira 14 miles West of Athens

Eleusis archaeological site contains a range of impressive Greco-Roman ruins, steeped in the richness of Greek mythology. Surrounded on all sides by a thriving modern industrial town, the site of Eleusis is renowned as the home of the Eleusinian mysteries, a series of annual initiation ceremonies for the cult of Demeter and Persephone which ranked among the most sacred religious rites of ancient Greece. The site was also the birthplace of Aeschylus, a playwright (or 'tragedian') who is known as the 'father of tragedy' and whose plays are still performed and read today. The Eleusis archaeological site houses a number of important ruins including the Sacred Court, a Roman reproduction of Hadrian's Arch in Athens and the Kallichoron Well, according to the Homeric Hymn, the resting place of Demeter…

The Ancient Sites of Greece

Kamiros on the Island of Rhodes

Kamiros (Kameiros) was an ancient city on the Island of Rhodes, the ruins of which include an acropolis. Excavations have revealed a long and diverse history at Kamiros including a temple to Athena dating to the 8th century BC. Twice destroyed by earthquakes (in 226 BC and 142 BC), the main remains at Kamiros date to the Hellenistic period, although some Classical elements are still visible. The Hellenistic city was built on three levels with various buildings and monuments including an agora, a Doric fountain house, a reservoir and a Stoa. Located on the Island of Rhodes's north-western coast, the other side of the Island from the more popular beaches, Kamiros is well worth a visit. It is easily accessible by car and less crowded than the better-known acropolis of Lindos. Unlike Lindos, the ancient city of Kamiros has not been overlaid by a modern town, so its geography remains visible to the visitor. The acropolis commands fabulous views across the sea to the coast of Turkey, and below it is, reasonably well preserved, the remains of a town with all its ancient conveniences…

The Ancient Sites of Greece

The Kerameikos archaeological site in Athens

Kerameikos is an archaeological site in Athens which contains the remains of an important ancient burial ground as well as a series of famous monuments. The site was once the home to the city's potters hence its name meaning pottery. Kerameikos also developed to become the site of a city cemetery. In fact, some of the oldest graves found at Kerameikos date back to as far back as the third millennium BC. It would continue to serve this function for centuries, including under the Romans right up to the sixth century AD. In addition to the burials Kerameikos, such as the Street of Tombs where prominent figures were laid to rest, the site also has the remnants of the entranceway to the ancient city of Athens. Visitors can see the ruins of what was the city wall, including the Sacred Gate and the Dipylon Gate. It is also where the Panathenaic procession, which was a great ancient Athenian festival that began its route from here. The ruins of the staging area for this procession called the Pompeion can still be seen at Kerameikos…

The Ancient Sites of Greece

The Ancient Agora on the Island of Kos

The Kos Ancient Agora contains a series of ruins dating from the fourth century BC to the sixth century AD. Amongst them are a temple, probably dedicated to Hercules, a shrine to Aphrodite and the columns of a Stoa or covered walkway dating from the third century BC. Over time, the Kos Ancient Agora would have been renovated and added to, including by the Romans. One such addition was a fifth century Christian basilica…

The Ancient Sites of Greece

Lato on the Island of Crete

The archaeological site of Lato in eastern Crete contains the ruins of an ancient city which once dominated this area. The city was built on top of two high hills that dominated the local area. The city went on to flourish throughout the Hellenic era. Lato was also the birthplace of Nearchos, the admiral of Alexander the Great. By the time of the rise of Rome, the city's harbour which was to the east of the city soon came to be of more prominence than the original settlement and slowly the institutions and administrative centre of the settlement were moved there, leaving the original city to slowly decline. Today the site is quite well preserved and contains the remains of houses, the agora, temples, ancient cisterns, basements, a theatre and a later threshing floor. The site has not been troubled by modern restorations and therefore contrasts very well with the more open construction of the Minoan Knossos Palace and Malia which are also located on the Island…

The Ancient Sites of Greece

The Lion Gate…

Mycenae in the Peloponnese Region of Mainland Greece

Mycenae is an important archaeological site in Greece. It was once the city at the centre of the Mycenaean civilisation of between 1600 BC and 1100 BC. Mycenae is located about 90 kilometres (56 miles) southwest of the city of Athens, in the north-eastern Peloponnese region. Argos is 11 kilometres (7 miles) to the south and Corinth is 48 kilometres (30 miles) to the north. The site is believed to have been inhabited since Neolithic times, Mycenae flourished into a fortified city and was ruled at one time by the famous King Agamemnon. At its peak, Mycenae was one of the most important Ancient Greek cities and is linked to several works of cultural significance, including the Odyssey and the Iliad. Today, Mycenae contains several well-preserved sites, including the Lion's Gate (see above) and the North Gate, which form parts of its fortified walls and which once stood 18 metres high and 6 to 8 metres thick. A few other dwellings can also be seen at Mycenae, together with a granary and some guard rooms. Other important structures include Mycenae's Terraced Palace, which was abandoned in the twelfth century. There are several burial sites but the most impressive of these burial sites and arguably the most remarkable of Mycenae's sites is the Tomb of Agamemnon, also known as the Treasury of Atreus. This once elaborate thirteenth century tomb is carved into the Mycenae hills…

The Ancient Sites of Greece

The Panathenaic Stadium in Athens

The site of the first modern Olympic Games in 1896, the 2,300-year-old Panathenaic Stadium in Athens is one of the most significant historical sites in Greece. Originally built around 330 BC, the ancient stadium was used to host the Panathenaic Games every four years. The stadium was rebuilt in the mid-second century AD by Herodes Atticus, a wealthy Greek-born Roman senator who built a number of grand public buildings in Athens at that time. The stadium, when first built, would have been able to accommodate around 50,000 people. Abandoned through the ages, it was not until the late 19th century that the stadium was excavated and subsequently rebuilt to host the reborn modern Olympic Games. As well as being a site of great historical importance, the Panathenaic Stadium now hosts modern competitions and famously hosted events at the 2004 Olympic Games. Today, the Panathenaic Stadium remains one of Greece's most significant and popular tourist sites and includes the annual culmination of the Athens marathon. People are, even today, allowed to use the stadium for their morning jog by jogging around the stadiums track…

The Ancient Sites of Greece

The Ancient Temple of Aphaea on the Island of Aegina

The ancient Temple of Aphaea on the Island of Aegina is one of the most important and picturesque temples in Greece. The site itself was the location of an important ancient sanctuary which dates far back into antiquity. The sanctuary was dedicated to the cult of Aphaia, a local deity later assimilated by Athena. Historical records and archaeological excavation have shown that a significant temple structure stood on the site in the 6th century BC and it is believed this earlier incarnation was destroyed by fire in 510 BC. The Temple of Aphaea ruins we see today date back to the second temple built on the site, which was constructed between 500 BC and 490 BC. Built in the Doric style, it comprised of twelve columns on each side while the internal temple (cella) had two rows of five columns each. The importance of the Aphaia sanctuary declined after the Athenians began to dominate Aegina from the middle of the fifth century BC. Some repairs were made to the temple in the fourth century, but by the end of the second century BC the area was largely abandoned. Today the Temple of Aphaea remains in a picturesque semi-ruinous state and is one of the most important ancient sites on the Island. Among the most interesting features of this ancient Greek temple was the pedimental sculptures, which show elements from history and legend. The east pediment showed elements from the first Trojan War, which was an early expedition by Herakles against the Trojan King Laomedon, and which included Telamon, son of Aiakos who was the first King of the Island. This expedition is not to be confused with the second Trojan War as described by Homer which is depicted on the west pediment and are of the three descendants of Aiakos called Ajax, Teukros and the now famous Achilles. As with other famous Greek sculptures, these pediments were removed in the 19th century and are now on display in the Glyptothek museum in Munich, Germany…

The Ancient Sites of Greece

The Temple of Bassae in the Peloponnese Region of Greece

The Temple of Apollo Epicurius at Bassae, also known simply at the Temple of Bassae, is not just beautifully preserved, but is often said to be one of the best examples of its kind in the Peloponnese. Built sometimes from the middle to end of the 5th Century (estimates range from 450-400 BC), the magnificent Temple of Apollo Epicurius is the highlight of the site of the former sanctuary of Bassae. Set amidst the rocky, mountainous and in a remote location, the Temple of Apollo Epicurius at Bassae is often praised for its unique blend of styles. The entire Temple of Bassae is now protected by a tent-like structure which help to protect the many wonderful architectural features of the temple…

The Ancient Sites of Greece

The Temple of Hephaestus in Athens

The Temple of Hephaestus is an imposing ancient Greek temple in the Athenian Agora area of Athens and was the site of worship of the Greek deity of fire, blacksmiths and sculpture. Built in the fifth century BC, the Temple of Hephaestus was later incorporated into the Church of Agios Georgios, this accounting for its excellent state of preservation…

The Ancient Sites of Greece

Temple of Poseidon of Sounio

The Temple of Poseidon of Sounio is a picturesque ruin of a fifth century BC Greek temple dedicated to the deity of the sea and is on the coast just 43 miles outside of the City of Athens. The temple is dramatically perched on a cliff overlooking the ocean, the Temple of Poseidon of Sounio is now made up of a rectangle of restored large Doric columns. The location gives the visitor truly spectacular views from this partially-ruined Greek temple which are hard to beat. The sunset, as seen from here, is one of the most spectacular in Greece. The site is roughly one hour's drive from Athens and there are several tour operators offering half-day trips to see the temple and enjoy the beautiful views…

The Ancient Sites of Greece

The Parthenon in Athens

The Parthenon is probably the most famous surviving site from Ancient Greece. Standing at the heart of The Acropolis in the centre of Athens. The Parthenon is a monument to Classical Greek civilisation and building techniques. Built during the golden age of Pericles the famous Athenian statesman the Parthenon was originally constructed to be a temple to the Ancient Greek goddess Athena. The Parthenon was built in the mid-fifth Century BC and replaced an earlier construction on the site which had been destroyed during the Persian Wars. Through the centuries, the Parthenon has also been used as a Christian Church and a Muslim Mosque. The Parthenon was heavily damaged in 1687 during a conflict between the Ottoman Empire and the Venetians. Many of the surviving sculptures from the Parthenon were removed from the site in the early 19th Century by the Earl of Elgin and are now on display in the British Museum. In recent years the Greek government has asked that the Elgin marbles be returned to Greece on many occasions but to-date all of their requests have been rejected by the British government…

The Ancient Sites of Greece

The Tombs of the Kings in Paphos on the Island of Cyprus

The Tombs of the Kings is a Hellenistic necropolis in Paphos on the Island of Cyprus that contains a series of eight well-preserved tombs. Given that the Tombs of the Kings is a third century BC site and the monarchy was abolished in 312 BC, the name is somewhat of a misnomer, but this does not detract from the visitor's experience. In fact, the name is said to derive from the impressive nature of the site. The Tombs of the Kings was the cemetery of the elite, including prominent figures and high ranking officials. It continued to be used throughout the Hellenistic and Roman periods up to the fourth century AD, possibly even by early Christians. However, as with many sites of this kind, in more recent times the Tomb of the Kings have been subject to looting and have also been used to quarry building materials. Furthermore, in medieval times, the Tomb of the Kings was damaged by squatters, some of whom apparently made changes to the tombs layout. Nevertheless, it is well worth visiting the Tomb of the Kings. The tombs are actually quite unusual for the area, being more Macedonian in architecture than to local styles. Visitors can wander down into the depth of these, mostly subterranean, rock tombs and view the atriums which still survive. The architecture of these tombs is quite impressive, some seeming more like houses than burial places. Sadly, very few of the frescoes which would once have adorned them survive, but you can still see fragments here and there. Well now that we have visited a selection of the ancient sites of Greece we will, in the next chapter, look at the modern history of Greece…

The History of Greece

The English name for the Hellenic Republic is Greece which comes from an ancient Latin word for that area. The word "Hellenic" derives from the word ancient Greeks used to refer to themselves. The word "Romeic" was also used to identify Greece in the past. The word comes from a medieval or Byzantine Greek term. Although Romeic was the most common self-designation used early in the nineteenth century, its use, has declined to be used in favour of the designation of Hellenic that has been used since that time. The words "Greek," "Hellenic," and "Romeic" refer not only to the country but also to the majority ethnic group. Greek culture and identity reflect the shared history and common expectations of all members of the nation-state, but they also reflect an ethnic history and culture that predates the nation-state and extend to Greek people outside the country's borders. Since 98 percent of the country's citizens are ethnically Greek, ethnic Greek culture has become almost synonymous with that of the nation-state. However, recent migration patterns may lead to a resurgence of other ethnic groups in the population in the future…

The History of Greece

The history of ancient Greece identified from archeological excavations have shown that the first settlements in Ancient Greece dates from the Palaeolithic era (11,000 to 3,000 BC). During the second millennium BC, Greece gave birth to the great stone and bronze civilisations of the Minoans (2600 to 1500 BC), the Mycenaeans (1500 to 1150 BC) and the Cycladic civilisation. These were the first important civilisations in the history of Greece. In the **Classical Period** (6th-4th century BC) Greece was very famous throughout the known world. The peak of the classical period is the 5th century BC, when the foundations of Western civilisation were created in Athens. This city-state became the greatest naval power of ancient Greece. This allowed all domains of culture, including philosophy, music, drama, rhetoric and even a new regime called democracy to arise. It is not an exaggeration to say that this period changed the history of the world. In ancient Greece Athens and Sparta were the most powerful city-states and the other city-states in the country were actually allied to one or the other of these two towns. In the 5th century, the allied Greek city-states managed to repel the **Invasion of the Persians.** However, the **Peloponnesian War** that followed, between Athens and Sparta, led to the decline of the glorious classical era of Greece. That was when the Kingdom of Macedon, a tribe residing in northern Greece, came to power defeating and conquering the other Greek city-states. After the death of King Phillip II, his son Alexander started a large expedition in Asia. In 334 BC, Alexander the Great invaded the Persian Empire. His army conquered all the surrounding lands as far as India. However, in 323 BC, he died in Babylon at the age of 33 and his Macedonian empire was torn apart and divided up with each segment being governed by one of his heirs…

The History of Greece

In 168 BC, the **Romans conquered Greece** and a new period started in the history of Greece. This is actually the time when ancient Greece turns into Roman Greece and so begins the modern history of Greece. At the beginning of the modern era the landmass of Greece becomes the field of many important battles and new cities are constructed, such as Nikopolis in western Greece. The city of Athens and generally the Greek culture starts to decline, but at the same time Greek becomes the second official language of the Roman Empire. The Romans read the works of the Greek classical philosophers and base their religion on the Olympian gods. In the 3rd century AD, the powerful Roman Empire starts to decline and is divided in two pieces, the Eastern and the Western Roman Empire. While the Western Roman Empire was gradually conquered by barbaric North-European tribes, the Eastern Roman Empire with Constantinople (Byzantium) as the capital developed (now called Istanbul) and changed into the **Byzantine Empire** that lasted for about 1,000 years. At this point of history, Christianity becomes the official religion of the new empire, new territories are occupied and new state laws are formed. These laws will later constitute the first laws of the Modern Greek state when it was formed in the 19th century. In 1453, the Ottoman Turks conquered Constantinople and gradually the rest of Greece, which had already partly been dominated by the Venetians and the Knights of Saint John. The country and its people suffered a great deal under the **Ottoman occupation** and frequent rebellions took place. As these revolutions were un-organised, they were all defeated by the Ottoman army that is until March 1821 when the **Greek War of Independence** broke out. The year 1821 is the cornerstone year in the modern history of the country we in the UK now call Greece. The country finally winning its freedom in 1829…

The History of Greece

The first independent Greek state was formed in 1829 and Ioannis Kapodistrias, a Greek diplomat in the Russian court was installed as the governor. The first Greek state, included the Peloponnese, Sterea and the Cyclades Islands. In 1831 Kapodistrias was assassinated, Prince Otto of Bavaria became the first King of Greece, followed by George I from Denmark in 1863. At the same time, the Ionian Islands were donated to Greece by Great Britain as a gift to the new King. The region of Thessaly was attached to the Greek state by the Turks. In the early 20th century, Macedonia, Crete and the Eastern Aegean Islands were also attached to the Greek state after the First World War. This was the time when the figure of an important Greek politician first appeared, Eleftherios Venizelos, the most famous Prime-Minister of Modern Greek history. The year 1922 was a troublesome year for Greece as many Greek refugees from Asia Minor came to the mainland, part of a population exchange with Turkey. Although at first, it was very difficult for the refugees to adapt to their new lives, they gradually contributed a lot in the development of the country. During World War II, Greece bravely resisted the Axis forces, but eventually most of the Greek territory was conquered by the Germans and in some parts by the Italians. After the Second World War, the Dodecanese Islands joined the nation after being under Italian occupation since the early 20th century. Three decades of political turmoil then followed, including a military junta from 1967 till 1974. Since 1975, the regime of Greece is a Parliamentary Republic. In more recent times Greece has joined the EU only to find that this has led to significant financial burdens being placed on its people. Time will tell how this will affect the nation in the long term. Greece is now a leading tourist destination worldwide…

The History of Greece

The Greece of Today

The population of Greece historically has been mobile. Sailors, shepherds, and merchants travelled as a matter of occupation, while peasants frequently moved in response to wars, land tenure policies, and agricultural needs and opportunities. Market towns such as Corinth and Athens have endured for millennia, but smaller settlements have appeared and disappeared with regularity. Over the last century, internal migration has overwhelmingly been from mountains to plains, inland to coastal areas, and rural to urban settlements. In this process, hundreds of new villages were founded while others were abandoned, and some towns and cities have grown greatly while others have declined. A strongly centralised settlement system revolving around the capital, Athens, has emerged from these moves. In Greece the population became predominantly urban after World War II, with only 25 percent living in rural settlements in 1991. With the concentration of economic opportunities, international trade, governmental functions, and educational and health facilities in only a few cities has led to the decline of many regional areas and the growth of Athens as the primary city of Greece. The population of Greece in February 2017 was 10.9 million…

The History of Greece

Kefalonia …

The Greece of Today

In 1991, Greater Athens contained 3.1 million people, a third of the population of Greece, while the next largest city, Thessaloniki, contained 396,000 people. There are distinctive regional architectural styles, in Greece such as the pitched roofs of the Arcadian mountains and the flat, rolled ones of the Cyclades. Until recently, much housing was small and owner-built from mud brick, stone, and ceramic tiles. Over the last fifty years, the use of industrially produced materials and the construction of more elaborate dwellings has accompanied a dramatic increase in commercial building. International architectural movements have also been influential. Rural settlements are still characterised by single-family houses, but urban areas contain apartment buildings of five to ten stories. A high value is placed on home ownership, and most urban apartments are owned, not rented. Families tend to buy or remodel their homes only after saving the funds needed to do so. There is a strong public-private distinction in spatial arrangements. Homes are considered private family spaces. Single-family houses often contain walled courtyards that have been replaced in urban apartments with tented balconies. plazas, open-air markets, shops, churches, schools, coffeehouses, restaurants, and places of entertainment are the major public gathering spots. In more recent times the rapid development of tourism in Greece has seen the explosion of hotel and apartment being built in Greece mainly on its many Islands. The success of Greece in attracting so many foreign visitors to its shores has meant that tourism is now a significant means of employment and wealth to its people. The history of Greece has played a significant and leading role in the development of civilisation. We all owe so much to this Mediterranean land of Greece. In the next chapter we will look at the key role religion has played in the development of Greece and its people…

The Religion of the Greeks

Today in Greece close to 98 percent of the people are Orthodox Christians, just over 1 percent are Muslims, and there is a small numbers of Jews, Seventh Day Adventists, Roman Catholics, and members of Protestant denominations. The Greeks became involved in Christianity very early. After the Roman Emperor Constantine embraced the new religion, he moved his capital to Constantinople in 330 AD. The new capital grew into the Greek-dominated Eastern Roman or Byzantine Empire. Tension between the Christian patriarchs of Constantinople and Rome ultimately led to the Schism of 1054, which divided the religion into Orthodoxy and Catholicism. The Orthodox Church represented and supported the Christian population of Eastern Europe after the Ottoman conquest. In 1833, after the revolution, the Orthodox Church of Greece became the first of several national Orthodox churches in the region, each autonomous while recognising the spiritual leadership of the patriarch in Constantinople. Today there are sixteen separate Orthodox churches and patriarchates. The Orthodox Church of Greece is officially designated the religion of the nation, its officials exert some influence in state matters, and it receives state funding. The Orthodox Church of Greece is overseen by the Holy Synod, whose president is the archbishop of Athens. Under this synod are regional bishops as well as monks, nuns, and priests who run specific churches and monastic institutions. Local priests are encouraged to marry, but other members of the clergy may not. Care of local churches is the responsibility of the community of worshipers, and priests are assisted by deacons, chanters, and local women who clean the buildings and bake the bread that is used in communion…

Religion in Greece

The Greek Orthodox religion includes a series of daily, weekly, and annual rites, including the Sunday liturgy and the Twelve Great Feasts, of which the most important is Easter and the Holy Week that precedes it. Twenty to twenty five percent of the population attends weekly services, while many more people are present at annual ones. There are four periods of fasting and saint's days in honour of the three hundred Orthodox saints. There are also rites associated with key events in the life cycle, such as funerals, weddings, and baptisms. Many people integrate religious practice into their daily lives, crossing themselves while passing a church or entering to light a candle, pray, or meditate. Greek Orthodox churches are often constructed in a cross in-square configuration, and all contain an icon screen separating the sanctuary where communion bread and wine are sanctified from the rest of the building. Icons are pictorial representations of saints in paint or mosaic that serve as symbols of holiness. In many Greek homes, there is a niche where icons and holy oil are displayed. Some churches and monasteries have become national sites of pilgrimage because of their association with miracles and historical events…

Religion in Greece

In Greek Orthodox belief, at the time of death, a person's soul begins a journey toward judgment by God, after which the soul is consigned to paradise or hell. Relatives wash and prepare the body for the funeral, which is held in a church within twenty-four hours of death. The body is buried, not cremated, for decomposition is considered part of the process by which a person's sins are forgiven and the soul travels to paradise. The next forty days are a precarious time, at the end of which the soul is judged. Visits are paid to the relatives of the deceased, and additional rituals are held, some with open displays of grief and singing of laments. Three to seven years after burial, the bones of the deceased are exhumed and placed in a family vault or a communal ossuary. The degree to which the body has decomposed and the bones have turned white is seen as evidence of the extent to which the person's sins have been forgiven and the soul has entered a blissful state. In Greece nearly all celebrations have a religious component, and all major rites of the Orthodox Church are public holidays. Among celebrations with a predominantly secular orientation are Ochi Day (28th October), commemorating the occasion when Greek leaders refused Mussolini's demand to surrender in 1940; Independence Day (25th March), when Bishop Germanos of Patras raised the Greek flag of revolt against the Ottomans near Kalavryta in 1821; New Year's Day, when people gather, play cards, and cut a special cake that contains a lucky coin; and, Labour Day (1st May), a time for picnics and excursions to the country…

Religion in Greece

Christmas in Greece

Christmas (Xristougenna), the Feast of the Nativity of Jesus is one of the most joyful days in the Greek Orthodox Church. Traditionally, the Christmas holiday period in Greece lasts 12 days, until the 6th January, which marks the celebration of the Feast of the Holy Theophany (Epiphany). There are many customs associated with the Greek Christmas holidays, some of which are relatively recent, "imported" from other parts of the world (like eating turkey on Christmas day and decorating the Christmas tree). In the past, Greeks decorated small Christmas boats in honour of St. Nicholas and today, they are increasingly choosing to decorate boats, instead of trees, reviving this age-old Christmas tradition. The singing of Christmas carols (or kalanda) is a custom preserved in its entirety to this day. On Christmas and New Year Eve, children go from house to house in groups singing the carols, accompanied usually by the sounds of the musical instrument "triangle," but also by guitars, accordions, lyres and harmonicas. Until recently children were rewarded with pastries but nowadays they are usually given money. In Greece hobgoblins are called "kallikántzari", friendly but troublesome little creatures which look like elves. Kallikantzari live deep down inside the earth and come to surface only during the 12-day period from Christmas until Epiphany. Throughout Greece, there are various customs and rituals performed to keep hobgoblins away. Kallikantzari disappear on the day of Epiphany when all water is blessed, and the hobgoblins return to the earth's core. Traditional culinary delights symbolize good luck in the New Year and adorn the white-clothed tables. Melomakarona (honey cookies) and Kourabiedes (sugar cookies with almonds) are the most characteristic and they characterise the beginning of the Christmas festivity. Another traditional custom that dates back to the Byzantine times is the slicing of Vassilopita (St. Basil's) pie or New Year's cake. The person who finds the hidden coin in his slice of the cake is considered to be lucky for the rest of the year…

Religion in Greece

Marriage Traditions in Greece

The Marriage traditions in Greece vary slightly from place to place. In the Islands you will find a more intensive and colourful tradition going on. In the Dodecanese, for example, the celebration starts a couple of days before when relatives and friends will go to the new house of the couple "to make the marriage bed". This is like the kitchen party found in some Western countries or similar to adding to the new couple's dowry. However, instead of gifts for the house, money (and sometime serious money) inside envelopes is given. Usually the couple's fathers will set the ball rolling by throwing money on the marriage bed as a gift to the new couple. Depending on their financial status, the amounts of money the fathers throw can sometimes be very large indeed. This is followed by friends and relatives who will add to this their envelope with money, afterwards a baby will be placed on the bed in order to bring prosperity and fertility to the couple. On the day of the wedding, from early in the afternoon, the two houses of the bride and groom's families will be very busy. At the bride's house, the bride's girlfriends will dress her and make her beautiful for the marriage ceremony, whilst at the house of the groom the main event of the preparations will be in full swing. As his friends are dressing him and getting him ready, the gathering of friends and family of the groom sing the marital song. A half hour before the ceremony people will go to the church. Traditionally musicians will follow as well, playing wedding songs, and this can still be seen today. At the gate of the church, the groom will wait for the bride and when she comes the ceremony will continue with a small liturgy, the exchanging of vows and the dance of Hisais. The Priest and the bride and groom must walk 3 times around the altar whilst the priest sings the Hisaie dance. The marriage ceremony is followed by a huge party. The best man or best woman of the bride and groom will also be the Godfather or Godmother of the first child that is born to the couple…

Religion in Greece

The Greek Orthodox religion does have some rules but, is more open than other denominations of Christianity. In Greece, a priest can marry (although this is not allowed for monks and bishops). Furthermore, following a divorce, Greeks can remarry in church. As a nation, although the Greeks are religious they are not seriously devout or fundamentalist in their approach to religious matters. The huge majority of Greeks will go only occasionally to the church for a service. This may be for a marriage, funeral or baptism. Everyone will go to the church on Good Friday and Easter Saturday partly to listen and follow the Liturgy but mainly for the spectacular firework displays that are a traditional part of a Greek Easter. Inside the church, the congregation will mostly consist of the older generation of especially women. Having said this, almost every Greek, young or old, will cross themselves when passing by a church and, in cases of danger and need, will cry out "help me Christ and Mary". Yes, the faith is deep and strong for almost every Greek even if they do not go to church often or do not take communion every Sunday leaving such religious rituals to once or twice a year. One of the main reasons for this is the Greek spirit of independence and freedom, a spirit which lives within every Greek soul. The Greeks have their strong faith in Christ and Mary but also do not want to be bound by rules that have been dictated by several emperors, patriarchs and monks of the old Byzantium era…

Religion in Greece

Traditions of the Greek Orthodox Religion

There is a main period of feasting that covers the 40 days before Easter week, the Sarakosti (the name derives from the number 40, Saranta). This feast starts at the end of the four week Greek Carnival time (Apokries) which begins around the middle of March on Clear Monday (Kathari Deftera). Clear Monday is the first Monday that follows the 4 weeks of Apokria. Even though the Greeks will not feast for the next 40 days, on this particular day, the Kathari Deftera, they will go to the countryside to celebrate with special feast food (Vegetables, Pickles, taramosalata, grilled octopus, lots of wine and the special flat bread made specially for this day (the Lagana). A part of the tradition beloved by children is kite flying. In the past, children often made their own kite for that day using newspaper, string and straws. Today the children buy plastic ready-made kites from the shops but the enjoyment and the tradition is still very much alive…

Religion in Greece

Traditions of the Greek Orthodox Religion

The Greek Feast of Klydonas and the act of jumping over fire during St John's celebration at the end of June is one of the traditions that has slowly disappeared. The reason why this is so is not surprising. As the cities got bigger and more crowded there was no longer anywhere that one could safely pile up logs and make a fire in the neighbourhood streets. 40 years ago though this was an exciting event that could be experienced in nearly every neighbourhood. A quaint tradition that happened the day before this Feast of Klydonas was for young unmarried girls to try and fish out of a jar of water a ring or coin that had been previously placed there. The Jar would be placed on the roof of buildings and covered by a white cloth and, the next evening, all the neighbours would gather at the doorstep of a house for the opening of the jar with the (Amilito Nero) the silent water. The young girls would fish around in the jar without being able to see deep into its contents, then as one girl was picking out of the jar a ring or a coin, an older woman would recite poems from the popular Almanac Calendar. These poems were a kind of prophecy for the girls and would ensure that they would find their true love to marry in the near future. This ceremony was followed with the jumping over the fire that had been lit in the middle of the street. Now that we have considered the religion of the Greeks we will, in the next chapter explore the geography of Greece…

The Geography of Greece

Greece is a peninsular and a very mountainous country located in Southern-Eastern Europe, in the Balkans peninsula. The country has the largest coastline in Europe (13,676 km) due to its numerous Islands. Greece has a total of 2,000 Islands but only 168 of these are inhabited. The country is washed to the east by the Aegean Sea, to the west by the Ionian Sea and to the south by the Mediterranean Sea. Two thirds of Greece is covered with mountains. The highest mountain peak is Mount Olympus, at an altitude of 2917 m. The country is very rich in natural resources providing petroleum, magnetite, lignite, bauxite, hydropower and marble. Over the years, the geography of Greece has influenced the development of many civilisations throughout the ages. Greece has a rich diversity in flora and fauna with many species that are unique to the country, which means that they are found only there in the world. These rare species are found in the forests, lakes, rivers, underground caves and canyons of Greece. In fact, the limestone and volcanoes found in Greece have helped the formation of many of these caves and canyons over time…

The Geography of Greece

The Meteora Monasteries Region of Mainland Greece

In the next few pages we be will looking at the characteristics of the geography of Athens, the capital of Greece, the different regions on the mainland and then we will journey to the Greek islands. Athens is the capital city of Greece. It belongs to the Prefecture of Attica, located at the centre of the Greek territory. Attica is actually a peninsula surrounded by four high mountains that form a basin. In this basin, the city and suburbs of Athens have been constructed. The extreme southern point of Attica is Cape Sounion, on top of which is an ancient temple dedicated to the god Poseidon. According to the myth, King Aegeus fell from Cape Sounion drowned himself, when he thought that his only son Theseus had been killed by the Minotaur on Crete. The western side of the Attica peninsula is divided by the Peloponnese region of mainland Greece that has the Corinth Canal, an artificial canal that was completed in 1893 and road bridges linking it to the rest of mainland Greece…

The Geography of Greece

The Greek mainland consists of the following regions: Sterea (Central Greece), Peloponnese, Thessaly (East central), Epirus (North West), Macedonia (North) and Thrace (North West).

Leros…

The Peloponnese is the most popular region of mainland Greece. It is located in the southern part of Greece and actually looks like an island connected to the mainland with two bridges: the bridge at the Corinth Canal and the cable bridge of Rio-Antirrio. The inland is dissected by high mountains that extend southwards towards a landscape of fertile plains, pine forested uplands and craggy foothills.

Greece also consists of many Islands and Island groups: Crete, Cyclades, Dodecanese, Ionian, Sporades and the Eastern Aegean Islands.

Chapel on the Island of Ikaria…

There are more than 2,000 large and small Greek Islands scattered both in the Aegean and the Ionian Sea. Most of them are located in the Aegean between the mainland and Turkey. The largest Greek Island is Crete and the second largest is Evia. Lesvos and Rhodes come next. Some of the best known and visited Greek Islands are Santorini, Mykonos, Rhodes, Crete, Thassos, Skiathos, Kefalonia, Zakynthos and Corfu…

The Geography of Greece

The Weather of Greece

The weather in Greece is fairly uniform throughout the mainland and the Greek islands. Due to its geographical position, Greece has mild winters and warm summers, cooled by different kinds of seasonal winds. The summers are characterised by sunshine and very little rainfall: great temperatures and lazy, restful and happy summer holidays are therefore guaranteed in Greece! The weather of the Aegean Islands and in the Ionian Sea is milder. Some regions of Greece are affected by the Meltemi, a summer wind which blows mostly over the Islands of the Aegean and offer perfect wind conditions for such holiday activities as sailing, windsurfing and kitesurfing…

The Geography of Greece

The Nature of Greece

Greece has a rich diversity to its nature. Located, as it is, on the crossroads of three continents (Europe, Africa and Asia), the landscape of the country contains a large a variety of flora and fauna. Two thirds of the country is mountainous and about 25% of the total land surface is covered with forest. These forests mostly consist of firs, oaks, poplars, plane trees and bushes. Some are aesthetic forests, like the Virgin Forests of Rodopi in Northern Greece, the Oak Forest in Foloi in the Peloponnese and the Black Fir Forest on the Island of Kefalonia. To help protect these forests from human activity, some of these regions have been made National Parks. Greece is largely composed of limestone rock, which has helped in the formation of many underground caves. A significant number of these caves have beautiful stalactites and stalagmites. There are many rare species of flora and fauna residing in the forests, caves and gorges throughout Greece. In fact, more than 6,000 plant species have been recorded in the country and 750 of them can only be found in Greece. The fauna of Greece is a rare mixture of European, Asian and African species. Many species are endemic, while others are migratory, particularly the bird species that stop off in Greece on their way from Northern to Southern countries. These migratory species create unique ecosystems in the lake and river deltas where they visit. The lakes and rivers are wonderful places for people to come and bird watch. The rivers of Greece tend to be relatively small but very turbulent and fast flowing making them ideal for sports like rafting, canoeing and/or river trekking. The large diversity and variety of the nature in Greece offers the visitor a delightfully rich experience. The best seasons to visit Greece to see its nature at its best is in the autumn and spring months, where the colours are wonderful and the weather is mild…

The Geography of Greece

The Wild Mammals of Greece

There are 116 species of mammals in Greece and 57 of them belong to endangered species, such as the Brown Bears of Epirus, wolves, snakes and other endangered species.

The Wild Birds of Greece

422 bird species have been recorded in Greece and about 70% of them are migratory birds.

The Domestic Animals of Greece

The most characteristic animals seen in Greece are the goat, sheep and cows. These domestic animals can be seen frequently in the Greek countryside, mostly in the mountains. It is a common experience to drive on the mountain roads and see sheep flocks getting in your way. The Greeks also keep cats and dogs…

The Geography of Greece

The Flora of Greece: Greece with its diverse climate and landscape has a rich and diverse collection of flora. Many species of trees, bushes, flowers and herbs grow all over the country.

The Forests of Greece: The Greek forest, as we have already seen, largely consist of fir trees, pine trees and bushes. These trees exist in the alpine parts of Greece, which are found in the northern part of the country and in high altitudes in Sterea and Peloponnese. Forests in lower altitudes mostly have poplars, plane trees, oaks and cypress trees. At the foot of the trees, various bushes and flowers grow.

The Cultivated Trees of Greece: The most characteristic tree of Greece is of course the olive tree. They can be seen all over the country, both on the mainland and on the many Islands of Greece. In fact, the olive oil is one of the most traditional products of Greece. The largest olive groves are found on the Island of Crete, the Peloponnese and on Lesvos Island, but generally visitors will see these trees everywhere in Greece. Greece also has an abundance of fruit trees, in particular orange, lemon, apple, pear, fig, peach, almond and walnut. Peach trees are largely cultivated in Naoussa Macedonia, cherry trees in Edessa, Kumquat in Corfu, strawberries in the Western Peloponnese, mastic trees in Chios Island and pistachio trees on the Island of Aegina.

The Vegetables of Greece: Vegetable cultivation is common in Greece, mostly tomatoes, cucumbers, zucchinis, eggplants and beans. Such cultivation in small quantities are frequently seen in the gardens of Greek houses and tavernas…

The Geography of Greece

Lake Tourlida at Messolongi in Greece…

The Flowers of Greece

In Greece there are many characteristic flowers to be seen such as: roses, daisies, poppies, orchids, lilies and a perfusion of various wildflowers. In fact, every region has special kinds of flowers growing in profusion.

The Greek Flora in Greek Mythology

It is interesting that various species of the Greek flora are mentioned in ancient Greek mythology. Hercules had to steal the golden apples of Hesperides on one of this labours. Daphne was turned into a laurel tree to escape from the love of god Apollo, Hades gave pomegranate seeds to Persephone to make her forget the Upper World and goddess Athena gave the olive tree to the residents of Athens.

The Lakes of Greece

Greece has many natural and artificial lakes and lagoons. Most of the lakes found in Greece are freshwater and were formed far from the coastline, either from tectonic forces or from the melting of snow on the mountains.

The Caves of Greece

Greece is a country with a rich geological structure and evolution, thousands of subterranean and underwater caves have been formed both on the mainland and on the Islands. Systematic explorations by geologists and speleologists all around the country have brought to light more than 8,500 caves, many of which are still unexplored…

The Geography of Greece

Farming in Greece

In recent years farms in Greece have started to modernise. Farming is an ancient activity in Greece and in fact the ancient Greeks traded their products and wine for luxurious fabrics and precious metals from other Mediterranean countries.

The Mountains of Greece

As we have already learnt Greece is primarily a mountainous country. The most significant range of mountains in Greece is called Pindus, forming the main mountain axis of the country, starting from Epirus and naturally extending through the Peloponnese and out as far As the Island of Crete. This mountain axis contains the highest peaks in the country. Mount Olympus in the Macedonia region is the highest mountain in Greece, reaching a height of 2,917 m (Mytikas peak). Olympus is world famous as the home of the Greek Gods. This is why they were also called the Olympian Gods. The mountains in Greece have a very rich biodiversity, rare scenery and unique forests. Various species of flora and fauna thrive in their forests and is why so many of them are protected as National Parks. These forests and the villages in the mountains create the perfect setting for autumn and winter holidays to Greece. In the mountains as well as skiing, many other sports can be practiced. In fact, there are many mountaineering and alpine clubs that offer organised activities in the mountains, from hiking, mountain biking and/or horse riding…

The Geography of Greece

The Rivers of Greece

The Rivers in Greece are relatively small in comparison to rivers found in many other countries. They start from the mountain tops where the snow melts, cross the valleys below and usually empty in the sea, or in some cases into lakes. The rivers in Greece are shallow and turbulent. The longest flowing rivers in Greece are Evros and Axios. However, they both originate from neighboring countries before flowing into the sea around Greece. The longest river that has its springs in the country is the Aliakmon River, which flows through western Macedonia. Apart from some sections of the rivers Evros and Loudias, the rest are not navigable due to the turbulence of the waters.

The Canyons and Gorges of Greece

Greece is dotted with a lot of canyons and gorges, both on the mainland and on the many Islands. The limestone landscape of the country was affected by rainfall and snow melting from the mountains that has resulted over many years, in the formation of large canyons. These canyons contain precious wild animals, birds, insects and other rare species. Vikos Gorge is a very impressive gorge in Greece and is located on the north western side of the country, in the region of Epirus near Zagoria. Vikos is the second deepest gorge in the world, after the Grand Canyon in the USA. On the Island Crete are the largest number of gorges in Greece. Crete has more than 250 small or large gorges. Some are crossed by rivers, some are totally inaccessible, while others are crossed by roads. The largest canyon in Crete is Samaria Gorge that takes about 6 to 7 hours to walk through from one side to the other…

The Geography of Greece

The Volcanoes of Greece

Greece has a large volcanic arch, which was created millions of years ago by the sinking of the African lithosphere (Oceania) under the Eurasiatic plate (mainland). This volcanic arch of Greece had an especially intense volcanic activity in the past that created the volcanic landscapes that we see in many regions and Islands around Greece. Most of the volcanoes in Greece and the Greek Islands are now extinct, however there are some still active. The most important active volcanoes in Greece are situated on the Islands of Santorini, Nisyros, Methana and Milos. They get thousands of visitors every year. In fact, volcanic hiking tours have developed for people with a special interest in volcanoes.

Active Volcanoes

The volcano on the Greek Island of Santorini is the most famous volcano in Greece. It has the largest caldera (crater) in the world with a height of 300 m and a diameter of 11 km. The special thing about this caldera is that it is actually sunken and filled with sea water. On the cliffs of the caldera, white sugar houses have been constructed offering breathtaking view. Boat tours depart from the old port of Fira on Santorini to visit the volcano, which is actually the island of Nea Kameni, formed by volcanic eruptions in the 16th century. The last eruption of the Santorini volcano was small and happened in 1950 and the volcano is still active. The second most famous volcano in Greece is located on the small island of Nisyros, Dodecanese. This is the youngest of the large volcanic centres in Greece, only 160,000 years old. In 1872, a large eruption happened and created a crater of about 6 to 7 meters. In 1888, another eruption happened forming a crater of 25 m diameter. In 1956, schisms emitting smoke was observed. Today the volcano is dormant. The largest crater that most tourists visit is Agios Stefanos, with a diameter and depth of 30 m…

The Geography of Greece

The Volcano at Methana

The peninsula of Methana, on the north eastern side of the Peloponnese, actually has 32 volcanoes that are mostly andesitic and dacitic lava domes. The volcanic activity in the peninsula started about one million years ago and in fact a large eruption took place in 230 BC. The last eruption of the Methana volcano happened in 1700. Today the volcano is dormant and many hiking and climbing tours are organized to the peninsula. Due to the volcanic activity, Methana also has famous thermal springs.

The Volcano at Milos

The volcano of Milos Island is also considered dormant. It is located in the centre of the island and has given the Island of Milos its richness in minerals and its strange geological formation. The last volcanic eruption on Milos took place in 90,000 BC. Other smaller volcanoes in Greece can be found on the Island of Kos and on the islet of Gyali, between Kos and Nisyros. In places were volcanoes exist, there are also thermal springs, such as Thermes Beach on Kos, the Thermals of Methana and the Hot Springs on the Island of Santorini…

The Geography of Greece

The Wine of Greece

Wine has been an important product in Greece since ancient times and in fact Greek wine was considered to be among the best in the Mediterranean basin, particularly in Roman times. This tradition is continued today. Almost every house in the villages of Greece has its own vineyard in the garden and produces a few bottles of wine every year. The most famous wine-producing region in Greece is Nemea in the Peloponnese. It has been famous for its high-quality wine since ancient times, Nemea has many wineries that open their doors to the public, particularly in autumn during the wine-pressing period. Other regions of the Peloponnese as well as Macedonia in Northern Greece also produce fine wine. As for the Greek Islands, Samos and Ikaria have produce high-quality wine since ancient times and this practice continues to this very day. Wineries are also found on the Islands of Kefalonia, Crete, Naxos, Paros and the Island of Santorini. The wine of Santorini has a very special spicy taste due to the volcanic elements of the soil and the water. Having look at some of the aspects of the geography of Greece, we will, in the next chapter discover the things that have contributed to the creatation of the unique civilisation we call Greek…

The Greek Civilisation

The location of Greece on the crossroads of three continents has had a dramatic effect on the Greek civilisation and culture. Using the Greek High School history books as an example, civilisation and culture began with the history of older civilisations like the Mesopotamian, the Middle East and Egypt and then moving on to incorporate Prehistoric Greece and Ancient Greek History. As a result, the Greeks took many elements from all these ancient civilisations around them, adapting the ones that were close to their nature and way of life whilst the remaining elements served to further develop and move them forward, like the development of astronomy, sculpture and architecture. Because of these developments a unique civilisation was created which always had the human at its very centre. From these things sprung the renowned Greek philosophy, democracy, the arts and sciences that are now featured in any major publication about ancient Greece. It was these things that were created by the ancient Greeks which was offered to the rest of human kind. Still today the Greeks do what their ancestors did 3000 years ago, they hold on to beliefs and ways of life learnt from the cultures of both the east and the west. The links with the East are still strong and the effect of Byzantine Greece can still be seen today in the Greek Orthodox religion, and in modern Greek music…

The Greek Civilisation

Greek Culture and the Traditions

The Ancient elements of Greek music can be found in the music of the Greeks of the Black sea (Pontos), in the ancient sound of the goat skin bagpipes (Tsampounes) on many Greek Islands, in the sounds of the flute of the Greek shepherds in northern Greece and in the sounds of the Cretan Lyra on Crete. All of these Byzantine and ancient elements come together with the Smyrneika. Smyrneika is the music that the Greeks of Asia Minor brought with them and is the most typical used in Greek folk music. However, as in the past so as today, the Greeks love to mix things, with the consequence that Greek music has adapted and adopted the musical elements from the West including Latin rhythms and sounds, Italian music, Rock and Blues as well as rap and hip hop music…

The Greek Civilisation

Greek owl cups

The Greek Language

Since language constitutes one of the most important elements of Greek culture and its best transmitter, it is interesting to see, in brief, how the Greeks speak today, how the Ancient Greek language became the modern language of today.

The First Written Language

The first written Greek letters were found on baked mud tablets, in the remains of the Minoan Knossos Palace on the Island of Crete. This language is known as Linear A and it has not been fully decoded. The most famous example of Linear A is written on the famous Phaestos Disc. In the 12th century BC, a new language started to develop, called Linear B, where each drawing symbol is a consonant-vowel combination. Linear B dates from the Mycenaean civilisation. In the late 9th and early 8th century BC, the language used was based on the Phoenician syllabary, written from left to right and back again. This form of inscription is the closest to the modern language of today…

The Greek Civilisation

The Greek Language - The Classical Period

During the Classical period (6th-4th century BC), the territory of Greece was divided into numerous states and each one had its own dialect. The two more important dialects were the Ionic and the Attic. During this period, Athens established itself as the political, economic and cultural centre of the Greek world, and therefore the Attic idiom started to be used as the common language. After the expeditions of Alexander the Great, Attic dialect was also expanded in the depths of the East and it was spoken by millions of people. This gradually led to a mixing of the dialect which was the beginning of the koine, or common dialect, mostly known as the Hellenistic koine. This type of language survived through the centuries and became an official language of the Roman Empire later on. The koine is the original language of the New Testament and the basis for the development of Medieval and Modern Greek. This language was further developed all through the Byzantine times…

The Greek Civilisation

The Greek Language - Katharevousa and Dimotiki

With the creation of the Modern Greek State in 1829, the question of the language, as an important part of the nation-building process, had to be resolved. After about four centuries of Ottoman occupation, Greece had mostly an oral culture due to all these centuries of different dominations. The question was the choice of language used in administration and education. One of the suggestions, to re-use the Attic language, was very attractive, especially because all the Western Europe was charmed by the Ancient Greek culture, and it would have been a great stimulus for the philhellenes. It proved impossible from a practical point of view. So, the Greek scholar Adamantios Korais (1748-1833), suggested to reform the spoken language of those times on ancient principals. This suggestion was accepted and the Katharevousa (meaning purified language) was created. The theme became politicised: a distinction rose between the Katharevousa, which became the high-style language associated with official functions such as governmental affairs, education and religion, and the Dimotiki language (popular language) which is used by Greek people in their everyday life…

The Greek Civilisation

The Greek Language - 20th century Greek language

In the 20th century, the Greek language debate took on a huge political significance: academics were sacked for using Dimotiki, riots were taking place in the streets and a lot of people were claiming that Katharevousa was being used as an instrument for denying access to education to the common people. Nationalist governments like the dictator of the Junta, Ioannis Papadopoulos, favoured Katharevousa. The issue was eventually solved in 1976 when the Dimotiki language was adopted in education and for administration purposes and has remained the formal language of modern day Greece. Most regions in Greece have their own local oral dialects and every region has, of course, its own local accent…

The Greek Civilisation

The Arts in Greece

The Greek Ministry of Culture supports all the Arts in terms of production, education, publicity, festivals, and national centres, such as the Greek Film Centre. There are provincial and municipal theatres, folklore institutes, orchestras, conservatories, dance centres, art workshops, and literary groups both on the mainland and on many of the Greek Islands. In Greece oral poetry and folk songs thrived even under Ottoman domination and developed into more formal, written forms as the nation-state emerged. Poets and novelists have brought contemporary national themes into alignment with the major movements in Western literature. There have been two Greek Nobel laureates: George Seferis and Odysseas Elytis. In Greece long-standing traditions of pottery, metalworking, rug-making, woodcarving, and textile production have been carried forward by artisan and craft cooperatives. Many sculptors and painters are in the vanguard of contemporary European art, while others continue the tradition of Orthodox icon painting. In Greece music and dance are major forms of group and self-expression, and genres vary from Byzantine chants to the music of the urban working class known as rebetika. Distinctively Greek styles of music, dance, and instrumentation have not been displaced by the popularity of Western European and American music. Some of the most commonly instruments used are the bouzouki, santouri (hammer dulcimer), lauto (mandolin-type lute), clarinet, violin, guitar, tsambouna (bagpipe), and lyra (a-stringed Cretan instrument), many of which function as symbols of national or regional identity. The popular Greek composers Mikis Theodorakis and Manos Hajidakis have achieved international fame…

The Greek Civilisation

The Arts in Greece

In Greece shadow puppet plays revolving around the wily character known as Karagiozis were very popular in the late Ottoman period. Dozens of theatre companies were founded in Athens, Thessaloniki, and other areas that performed contemporary works and ancient dramas in Modern Greek. Films are a popular form of entertainment, and several Greek filmmakers and production companies have produced a body of melodramas, comedies, musicals, and art films. The University of Athens was established in 1837, with faculties in theology, law, medicine, and the arts (which included applied sciences and mathematics). Further education in Greece is very important and there is a national system that has expanded to nearly twenty public universities and technical schools that offer a full range of academic and applied subjects. There are several state-funded research centres, such as the National Centre for Scientific Research, the National Centre for Social Research, and the Centre for Programming and Economic Research…

The Greek Civilisation

Culture in Greece

There is a large variety of cultural events in Greece that are organised in Athens, other cities and on the Greek islands. Some of these events are:

The Athens Epidaurus Greek Festival

The Athens Epidaurus Greek Festival takes place every summer (from June to August) and includes various performances, like modern theatre, ancient drama, ballet, opera, jazz and classical music concerts and art exhibitions. The events take place in various theatres around Athens and in the Ancient Theatre of Epidaurus. In fact, the peak of this festival is the ancient drama performances that are displayed in summer weekends in Epidaurus.

The International Film Festival of Thessaloniki

The International Film Festival of Thessaloniki is one of the most important cultural events in Greece. It takes place every November and it works as a stand for new directors to present their work.

The Rockwave Festival

The Rockwave Festival takes place every June and welcomes international bands and musicians. The rock concerts are presented in the Rockwave Scene in Malakasa, about 40 km north of Athens. The festival lasts for three days and concerts are performed all day long, from morning till midnight…

The Greek Civilisation

The Greeks do Love their Football…

The Sani Festival

A yearly celebration since 1993, bringing together nationally and internationally acclaimed artists at Sani Halkidiki. Events, such as music concerts, dance performances and painting exhibitions, are held in different venues around the Sani Resort from July to September.

The Megaro Gyzi Festival

The Megaro Gyzi Festival takes place every August on the Island of Santorini. It includes music concerts, performances, art exhibitions and lectures that take place in Megaro Gyzi Cultural Centre in Fira on Santorini.

The Naxos Festival

The Naxos Festival takes place every July and August in Bazeos Tower on the Island of Naxos. It includes musical concerts, theatre performances, art exhibitions, lectures and art workshops. There is a large range of other cultural events and festivals take place all around Greece and the Greek Islands. Most festivals are organised in the summer months.

Having explored the civilisation of Greece in the next chapter we will consider the Greek Economy…

The Economy of Greece

Greek Food and Drink

The high volume of visitors to the shore of Greece make the money earned through the sale of food and drink is a vital economic source of revenue for the people of Greece. When it comes to food in Greece the diet mainly consists of grain, grapes, and olives which are central to the diet, supplemented with eggs, cheese, yogurt, fish, lamb, goat, chicken, rice, and fruits and vegetables. In Greece certain foods are emblematic of the national identity, including Greek salad, moussaka, baklava, thick coffee, and resonated wine (*retsina*). Coffee-houses have long functioned as daily gathering places for men. Any Greek will tell you that you should always find time for a coffee. Dining out has gained in popularity, in recent years, with a corresponding increase in the number and variety of restaurants and tavernas. Greeks believe that guests must always be offered refreshment, and in Greece all major ceremonies involve food. At funerals, mourners are given koliva (boiled wheat, sugar, and cinnamon), a special cake is baked on New Year's Day, and the midnight Easter service is followed by a feast, generally of lamb…

The Economy of Greece

The Politics of Greece

The conventional short form of the country's name is Greece (Hellas or Ellada). Its official name is the Hellenic Republic (Elliniki Dimocratia). The capital of Greece is Athens. Since the Constitution was signed in 1975, after the military junta of 1967 to 1975 and a referendum which rejected the monarchy, the newly built democratic Greek system was created which is a parliamentary republic with the President of the Greek Republic as the head of the state, appointed by legislative power. The President of the Hellenic Republic is the chief of the state. He is elected by the Parliament for five years and his service can be renewed for another five years. He appoints the prime minister. The Cabinet is appointed by the president on the recommendation of the prime minister. The legislative power is held by the Parliament, called "Vouli ton Ellinon". The Parliament has 300 seats and its members are elected every four years with elections. In Greece voting is compulsory for citizens older than 18 years. The judicial power is organised as followed: Supreme Judicial Court and Special Supreme Tribunal are formed by judges appointed for life by the president, after he has consulted a judicial council. The legal system is based on a codified Roman law and is judiciary divided into civil, criminal and administrative courts. Greece has few major international political disputes however, the problem of their relations with Turkey is an ongoing issue. In fact, territorial, maritime and air disputes are very frequent between the two counties. The Cyprus Issue does not help the situation. The other big international dispute is with the Former Yugoslav Republic of Macedonia, a dispute that concerns the name of Macedonia. Greece is part of many International organisations, such as NATO (since 1952) and the EU (since 1981)…

The Economy of Greece

The Greek Economy

Although the economy of Greece had improved in recent decades due to the industrial development and tourism, presently the country faces a large and severe economic crisis. The currency of money in Greece since January 2002 is the euro, which replaced the drachma. The preparation for the Olympic Games of 2004 gave an impulse to the Greek economy. However, presently the country faces a severe debt crisis and has many challenges to face, such as the low rate of development and the large rate of unemployment (25% in December 2012). The Greek economy is based on the service sector (85%) and industry (12%), while the agricultural sector consists only 3% of the national economic output. The most important economic industries in Greece are tourism and merchant shipping. In fact, about 15 million international tourists visit Greece every year, which makes it the 7th most visited country in the EU and the 16th in the world. Greece has the largest merchant marine shipping fleet in the world that provides 16% of the world's total capacity. Greece is also a member of the International Monatery Fund, the World Trade Organisation, the Organisation for the Economic Co-operation and Development and many other world financial organisations. Following the 2007 world financial crisis, the Eurozone debt crisis and the long term problems of the Greek economy, Greece presently faces significant problems, like the high rate of unemployment (25% in December 2012), tax avoidance and corruption of its political parties. As a result, the country received (April 2010) a large loan from the World Monetary Fund and the European Union. In exchange for this large bailout, to deal with this problem the government announced combined spending cuts and tax increases on top of the tough austerity measures already taken…

The Economy of Greece

The History of the Greek Economy

In Greece farming, herding, fishing, seafaring, commerce, and crafts were the historical mainstays of the economy. Before the establishment of the modern state, most people were poor, often landless peasants who worked on feudal-like estates controlled by Turkish overlords and Orthodox monasteries. As the Ottoman Empire faced competition from the economies of Western Europe, some peasants began producing cash crops such as currants and lumber for sale to England and France, shipbuilders carried produce from the Black Sea to the Atlantic coast, and carpet makers and metal workers sold their wares throughout Eastern and Central Europe. After the revolution, the nation was deeply in debt to foreign creditors and lacked the capital and infrastructure needed for economic development, nor could it compete with the increasingly industrial economies of Western Europe. Families produced most of their own subsistence needs, from food to housing, while engaging in a variety of entrepreneurial activities, producing everything from sponges and currants to tobacco and cotton. The weakness of the economy and the unpredictability of foreign markets led to periods of economic crisis that sparked large-scale emigration by the late nineteenth century…

The Economy of Greece

The History of the Greek Economy

In the twentieth century, industry was strengthened by the influx of urban refugees after the Catastrophe of 1922 but it remained a relatively small sector of the economy. The growth spurred by foreign aid in the 1950's and 1960's was followed by high inflation rates in the 1970's and 1980's. Governmental efforts at economic stabilisation and payments from the European Union brought inflation down to 4 percent by the late 1990's. Current economic efforts are focused on industrial development, effective taxation collection, downsizing of the civil service, keeping inflation in check, and resolving the national debt and dependence on European Union payments…

The Economy of Greece

Greece of Today

In the past in Greece, legislation was passed that distributed large agricultural estates to peasant families, most farmland came to be owned by the people who worked it by the early twentieth century. Population growth and inheritance practices have produced small individual holdings, often scattered in several plots at a distance from each other. Much grazing land is publicly held, although herders pay fees and establish customary use rights over particular sections. The previous mainly subsistence economy activities dwindled during the twentieth century. Today handmade crafts are generally aimed at the tourist trade, farming is oriented toward sale, and some basic foodstuffs are now imported. In Greece family members often now engage in a variety of cash-producing activities, combining commercial farming with earning wages in factories, or tavernas, the renting of rooms to tourists or undertaking construction work, or sailing in the merchant marine or driving a taxi. In Greek families a high value is placed on economic flexibility, being one's own boss, and family-run enterprises. The most common means of earning a living today are in the construction industry, tourism, transportation, and small-scale shop keeping. Major cash crops grown include tobacco, cotton, sugar beets, grains, vegetables, fruits, olives, and grapes. Herders produce meat, milk products, wool, hides, and dung for sale. Fishing contributes little to the gross domestic production earnings whilst mining produces lignite, bauxite, asbestos, and marble for sale both at home and abroad…

The Economy of Greece

Greece of Today

In Greece industrial manufacturing contributed 18 percent to the GDP (gross domestic product) in the 1990's and employed 19 percent of the labour force. The major products of Greece are textiles, clothing, shoes, processed food and tobacco, beverages, chemicals, construction materials, transportation equipment, and metals. In Greece small enterprises dominate. In Greece the international balance of trade has long been negative. The country exports manufactured products (50 percent of exports), agricultural goods (30 percent), and fuels and ores (8 percent), and imports manufactured products (40 percent of imports), food (14 percent), fuels and ores (25 percent), and equipment (21 percent). In the 1990's, trade increasingly focused on European Union countries, with the major partners of Greece being Germany, Italy, France, and Britain, followed by the United States. The negative trade balance is offset by "invisible" sources of foreign currency such as shipping, tourism and European Union payments for infrastructure development, job training, and economic initiatives. The Greek merchant fleet is still the largest in the world and tourism brings up to eleven million foreign visitors to its shores every year…

The Economy of Greece

Greece of Today

In Greece the primary sector (farming, herding, and fishing) contributes over 8 percent to the gross domestic product (GDP), the secondary (mining, manufacturing, energy, and construction) sector contributes over 23 percent, and the tertiary sector (trade, finance, transport, health, and education) contributes 68 percent. The primary sector employs 22 percent of workers, the secondary sector 28 percent, and the tertiary sector 50 percent. Immigrants constitute 5 to 10 percent of the labour force in Greece. Society in Greece despite income differences in the population and a small upper stratum of established families in the larger cities, the class system has been marked by mobility since the establishment of the modern state. Former bases of wealth and power disappeared with the departure of the Ottomans and the dismantling of agricultural estates. A fluid class system fits the strongly egalitarian emphasis of the culture. The degree to which minority groups receive the rights and opportunities of Greeks is a topic of much public discussion. The fluidity of class and status in Greece means that symbols of social stratification are changeable and diverse, although the trappings of wealth can convey a high position in society, as do owning your own home or being fluent in foreign languages and adopting Western ways and styles…

The Economy of Greece

Greece of Today

As previously mentioned Greece is a parliamentary republic modelled on the French system. The redrawn constitution of 1975 established a single legislative body with three hundred seats. The president serves as the ceremonial head of state, while the prime minister is the head of government. Voting is mandatory for those Greeks over eighteen years of age. A large civil service bureaucracy administers a host of national, provincial, and local agencies. Governmental functioning often is described as hierarchical and centralised. A municipal reorganisation in 1998 combined smaller communities into larger ones in an effort to strengthen the power of local government. Greek political history has been marked by frequent moments of uncertainty, and there have been several military coups and dictatorships, the last being the junta that reigned from 1967 to 1974. Since the end of the junta, two major parties have alternated in power: New Democracy, which controlled parliament from 1974 to 1981 and from 1989 to 1993 and the Panhellenic Socialist Movement (PASOK), which controlled it from 1981 to 1989 and from 1993 to the present day. Citizens of Greece maintain a wary scepticism toward politicians and authority figures. Support in national elections often was garnered through patronage, extensive networks of ritual kin, and personal ties dating back to the nineteenth century. Local-level politics operate differently from politics on the national level. Municipalities elect leaders more on the basis of personal qualities than political affiliation, and candidates for local office often do not run on a party ticket. Dealing with the large civil service bureaucracy is seen as a matter for creativity, persistence, and even subtle deception. Individuals often are sent from office to office before their affairs are settled. Those who are most successful operate through networks of personal connections…

The Economy of Greece

Greece of Today

In Greece the legal system is based on modified Roman law, with strong protection for the rights of the accused. There are criminal, civil, and administrative courts, and since 1984, the police force, which previously was divided into urban and rural units, has operated as a single force. There is little violent crime in Greece. Tax evasion often is considered the most serious legal concern. Peer pressure, gossip, belief in forces such as the evil eye, and the strong sense of proper behaviour and social responsibility all operate as informal mechanisms of social control. The continuing disputes with Turkey and Macedonia and horrible experience of past wars that all form important parts of social memory in Greece, but since the Civil War there has been a different climate, especially since the end of the Cold War and the removal of foreign troops from its shores. Greece stills spends a high percentage of its budget on the defence industry. The Hellenic Armed Forces are divided traditionally into an army, an air force, and a navy. There is a universal draft of all males at age twenty for eighteen to twenty-one months of service, with some deferments and exemptions. There are 160,000 soldiers on active duty and over 400,000 reservists at any one time. Greece has an extensive social welfare system. There is a national health care system and a state-directed system of disability and pension payments. There are over 650 different pension programs, with membership depending on type of work undertaken. The government also has a system of earthquake and other disaster compensation. Banks have been established to support particular sectors of the economy. Caring for the personal needs of the elderly, infirm, and orphaned is considered a family responsibility…

The Economy of Greece

Greece of Today

In Greece today there are many voluntary organisations including hobby clubs, scouts, sports organisations, performance ensembles, environmental groups, craft cooperatives, and political pressure groups. Among the most common are urban-based organisations formed by people from the same rural area. For example these associations enrol as much as one-quarter of the Athenian population and raise funds and exert political pressure on behalf of their areas of interest. Agricultural cooperatives are widespread in Greece, enabling family-based farmers to buy and sell in bulk. Trade unions in Greece are less well established. In Greece rural men and women traditionally shared agricultural tasks, doing some jointly and dividing others by gender. Land and property have long been owned by both men and women, with husbands and wives contributing fields to the family. As the population became urbanised, this pattern shifted. Among families that operated small shops and workshops, both men and women remained economically active. Among those who sought employment outside the home, women were more likely to work at lower-paid positions and to stop working when they have children. Open access to education and evolving child care arrangements are changing this situation, and women now constitute 45 percent of the paid workforce. In Greece gender roles were relatively differentiated and male-dominant until recently. Traditionally, men were associated with public spaces and women with private, with the major exception of the role played by women in attending, cleaning, and maintaining churches. There were nevertheless many arenas in which women asserted power or operated in a female-centred world. Their economic role in the family; ownership of property; position as mother; wife, and daughter; maintenance of the household; religious activities; and artistic expression through dancing, music, and crafts all totally involve women…

The Economy of Greece

Greece of Today

There has been a dramatic decline in gender differentiation in the last few decades. Women received full voting rights in 1956, and the Family Law of 1983 established legal gender equality in family relationships and decision making. A majority (53 percent) of students in universities are women, and the percentage of women in public office has also increased. Women are now fully present in public spaces, including restaurants, nightclubs, beaches, stores, and public plazas. Marriage in Greece, as already mentioned, is considered the normal condition of adulthood. With the exception of monastic orders and the upper echelons of the clergy, nearly all people in Greece marry. Arranged marriages in which parents negotiated spouses, dowries, and inheritance for their children were once common but have recently declined. Marriages are monogamous, and the average age of marriage in Greece is the late twenties for women and the mid-thirties for men. The divorce rate is among the lowest in Europe. Until 1982, all marriages occurred in churches, but civil marriages have been legal since that time. It is common in Greece for elderly parents to join the household of one of their adult children. Sons and daughters receive roughly equivalent shares of their parents' wealth in the form of fields, housing, money, higher education, and household effects. Daughters generally received their portion at marriage, but the Family Law of 1983 made the formal institution of the dowry illegal. However, there continues to be considerable transfer of property from parents to children when the children marry. The family-based household unit is the most important kinship group in Greece. Ritual kin in the form of godparents and wedding sponsors retain a special relationship throughout a person's life…

The Economy of Greece

Baptism Oils…

Greece of Today

In Greece midwives were common until the mid-twentieth century, but most babies are now born in hospital. Babies are showered with overt displays of affection by male and female relatives. There is special concern over feeding and a belief that children need to be coaxed into eating. The central ceremony of infancy is baptism, which ideally occurs between forty days and a year after birth. This ceremony initiates the baby into the Greek Orthodox community and is the moment at which a baby's name is officially conferred. For Greeks the successful establishment of one's children is a driving goal. Parents willingly make sacrifices for their children, and there is a continuing emotional bond between parents and children. Both parents are actively involved in child rearing, along with grandparents and other relatives. Adults give children freedom to explore and play, cultivate their abilities to converse and perform, and participate in social occasions. Parents also stress the value of education. The public school system was established in 1833, and 95 percent of the population is literate. Schooling is compulsory in Greece and free for the first nine years and optional and free for the next three. Over 90 percent of students attend public schools. In Greece higher education is strongly valued. There is a state run university, technical, and vocational school system whose capacity is currently short of demand. Entrance is achieved by nationwide examinations, and many secondary school students attend private afternoon lessons to prepare them for these tests. In the 1990's, 140,000 students annually vied for 20,000 university seats and 20,000 technical college seats. Many students ultimately seek further education abroad…

The Economy of Greece

Greece of Today

In Greece much of an individual's social life takes place within a close circle of family and friends. Group activities revolve around eating, drinking, playing games, listening to music, dancing, and animated debate and conversation. These gatherings often aim at the achievement of kefi, a sense of high spirits and relaxation that arises when one is happily transported by the moment and the company. Drinking may contribute to the attainment of kefi, but becoming drunk is considered disgraceful by Greeks. A major occasion on which people open their homes to a wide range of visitors is the day honouring the saint for whom a person is named after. On those days, it is permissible to call on anyone bearing that saint's name. Guests generally bring sweets or liquor, and the honorees treat their visitors to food and hospitality. In Greece hospitality is seen as both a pleasure and a responsibility. Hosts are generous, and guests are expected to accept what is offered with only token protests. Hospitality is often extended to foreigner visitors. As mentioned previously the state-run National Health Service, a network of hospitals, clinics, and insurance organisations, was established in 1983. The service provides basic health care even in remote areas, but there is an over concentration of hospital facilities, doctors, and nurses in Athens and other major cities on the mainland of Greece. Private health care facilities are used by those who can afford them. The health status of Greek citizens is roughly equivalent to that of Western Europe. Western concepts of biomedicine are well accepted but are supplemented for some individuals by longstanding cultural conceptions concerning the impact that certain foods, the wind, hot and cold temperatures, envy, the evil eye and anxiety have on health and well-being…

Greece at its Best

Greece and the Greek Islands are known for three things: ancient civilisations, amazing landscapes and great beaches. Really beloved by people, Greece is so rich in culture and beauty that it never seems to be completely explored, no matter how many times you visit it. After all, this is one of the reasons that has seen Greece listed as one of the top twenty tourist destinations worldwide every year. This is because Greece, has such beautiful nature, sensational beaches, mild climate, clean sea and very friendly people all of which encourages people to come back to the shores of this wonderful land every summer. Greece is a dreamy country on the eastern side of the Mediterranean Sea. Among the most popular destinations in the world, tourists keep coming to Greece to enjoy the hot sun, the exotic beaches, the famous hospitality of the locals and the interesting sightseeing. This is a country with a long history and rich culture, with many beautiful places to visit. One trip is never enough to see the country. There are so many fabulous Greek Islands and mainland places that it takes many trips to see just a small part of Greece. Every Island and every mainland region has a special beauty all of its own to offer. Greece is world famous for its amazing beaches. Sandy or pebbled, organised or secluded, beaches in Greece are ideal for all tastes. The most impressive beaches are found in the Cyclades and the Ionian islands, such as Myrtos Beach on Kefalonia, Navagio Beach on Zakynthos, Porto Katsiki Beach on Lefkada and Super Paradise Beach on Mykonos. Every year, the Greek beaches are rated amongst the most beautiful and clean beaches in the world…

Greece at its Best

Balos Beach in Chania on the Island of Crete

Balos is amongst one of the best beaches in Greece and is just one of the most beautiful beaches on Crete. It is 60 km North West of the town of Chania. When looking down from the surrounding hills the beach of Balos has white sand, soft seabed and crystal clear seawater. Opposite the beach, there is a rocky Island called Gramvoussa. On the top of this island, there is a Venetian castle that has gorgeous views of the surrounding area and out to sea. The beach at Balos is reached by 10 km rough track from Kaliviani, a village close to Kissamos. Visitors will either need a four wheel drive car or alternatively visitors can go to the beach by taking an excursion boat from Kissamos…

Greece at its Best

Myrtos Beach on the Island of Kefalonia

Myrtos Beach is without doubt one of the most visited and beautiful beaches on Kefalonia. It is located 30 km north of the Island capital of Argostoli, in a beautiful area surrounded by high verdant hills. Myrtos beach has gained a worldwide reputation, been used by filmmakers (Captain Corelli's Mandolin) and has been featured constantly in travel magazines as being among one of the best beaches in Greece and in the world. It has received many awards for its cleanness and its natural beauty. The beach is a bay that is a semi-circular shape surrounded by impressive white rocky cliffs with lush vegetation on top of them creating a very spectacular setting. Mythos Beach is surrounded by lush green vegetation, steep hillsides, a beach of white pebbles and the crystal clear seawater. All of which makes for stunning scenery. The beach has the usual array of umbrellas and sunbeds while a small part remains completely un-cluttered and un-spoilt and is therefore, ideal for people who want to just lay on a towel and sunbathe. The natural beauty of Myrtos is the trademark of Kefalonia and is one of the most photographed places in Greece. The beach however, can be affected by strong winds at certain times. Myrtos also offers spectacular sunset views. On the beach visitors have access to a wide range of facilities and a nice snack bar offering much needed cold drinks. Myrtos is easily accessed by all means of transport. While you are descending to the beach, you will enjoy some amazing views…

Greece at its Best

Porto Katsiki Beach on the Island of Lefkada

Porto Katsiki Beach is one of the best beaches on the Island of Lefkada and among the ten best beaches of Greece and anywhere else in the Mediterranean for that matter. It is located 45 km southwest of the Island's capital and close to Athani village. The natural beauty of Porto Katsiki offers the visitor one of the most impressive sights that Lefkada has become famous for. Abrupt white cliffs form a wild yet magnificent backdrop to the beach and the deep blue seawater of the Ionian Sea. Lush vegetation covers the surrounding area creating one of the most idyllic landscapes in the world. Numerous sunbeds and umbrellas cover this famous sandy beach but the cliffs offer some beautifully shaded spots for some privacy and relaxing sunbathing. Steps lead directly to the beach. Porto Katsiki is simply irresistible for many thousands of visitors from around the world and a unique sightseeing experience. It is also visited by many private yachts which is simply the best way to access this wonderful beach. It can also be reached by using a car. Visitors can also use a taxi-boat from the villages of Vassiliki and Nidri to reach the beach. Car parking, bars and tavernas are located at the top of the stairs leading up from the beach…

Greece at its Best

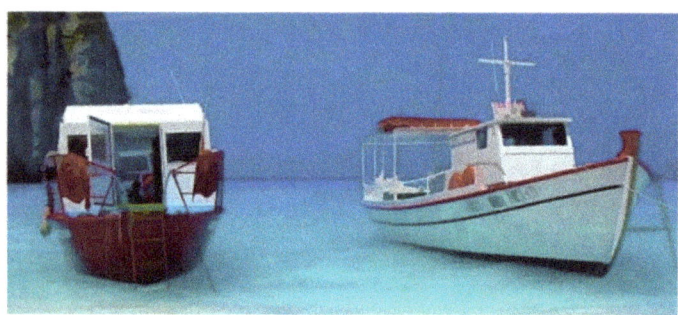

Shipwreck Beach or Navagio Bay Beach on the Island of Zakynthos

The beach of Navagio or Shipwreck cove is the most famous beach on Zakynthos lying on the western side of the Ionian Island, close to Anafotiria village. The Shipwreck on the beach is one of the most photographed landscapes in Greece. It is considered, by some, as one of the best beaches in Greece. It was initially called Agios Georgios but owes its new name to the shipwreck of a boat that was transporting a cargo of illegal cigarettes, in 1983. The ship was washed ashore and left high and dry. As the years passed, the sand completely surrounded the ship and now it looks as if it emerges from it. The vestiges of the ship can be seen in the middle of the large white sand and pebble beach which has amazing turquoise and crystalline seawater. The beach has huge vertical cliffs of white rock surrounding it that creates a unique and enchanting image. To reach this paradise, you will have to take a little boat from the small port of Porto Vromi. These taxi boats leave every hour and the trip takes about 30 minutes…

Greece at its Best

Kyra Panagia Beach Karpathos

This beautiful sandy beach lies in a small cove right between the mountains and has a fine mixture of white sand and smooth pebbles, and crystalline seawater. It is located 14 km north of Pigadia, the capital of Karpathos and close to Apella beach. The beach is considered to be one of the best beaches in Greece. The beach offers an amazing swimming experience with a striking mountain backdrop. It is reachable by car or by boat from Pigadia. There are a few apartments, an hotel as well as a fish tavern nearby. On Kyra Panagia beach there are the usual umbrellas and sunbeds available for hire…

Greece at its Best

Agios Prokopios Beach on the Island of Naxos

The beach is located some 5 km away from the capital, Agios Prokopios is one of the most popular beaches on Naxos and considered to be one of the most beautiful beaches in Greece and Europe. The long golden sandy beach extends for over 1.5 kilometres and has beautiful crystalline seawater and is protected from the strong winds frequently blowing onto the Island. One part of the beach offers sunbeds, umbrellas and water sports facilities whereas the other part of the beach is left to its natural beauty and totally unspoiled by tourist facilities. The beach is backed by dunes and, behind them lies a small village which offers some hotel accommodation, restaurants, tavernas, cafes and bars. Agios Prokopios can be reached by local buses that leave frequently from the capital, Naxos Town…

Greece at its Best

Super Paradise Beach on the Island of Mykonos

Super Paradise Beach is located right next to Paradise Beach and is reachable by water taxi-boat (regular boat services are available from Platis Yialos) and by using the local bus. It is considered to be one of the most beautiful beaches in Greece. Mykonos Super Paradise is less organised than neighbouring Paradise and has beautiful crystalline seawater and soft golden sand. Whilst it is true that this beach may not suit everyone tastes which is largely due to the fact that Super Paradise Beach is the most famous homosexual beach of Greece, attracting homosexuals and heterosexuals from all over the world. Due to its popularity, Super Paradise Beach can get very crowded during the peak summer season…

Greece at its Best

Valtos beach of Parga

Valtos beach is found to the west of Parga, down the hill where a Venetian castle was built. It takes just a 20-minute walk to get there from the town and it is also accessible by car, bicycle or obviously by boat. It is considered to be one of the best beaches in Greece. There is a water-taxi service from Parga harbour to Valtos beach in the summer months. Valtos Beach extends along 3 km of coastline so no matter how crowded it gets, there is always room for everyone. The beach has small, soft pebbles and is surrounded by greenery and clear, deep seawater. Valtos beach is a nice place to swim, sunbathe and have a relaxing day by the seaside. Walking on the beach at Valtos in the evening or early in the morning, is highly recommended. There are many tavernas and cafes at Valtos beach that are open all day. The resort also has some small hotels and rooms to rent…

Greece at its Best

Simos Beach on the Island of Elafonissos

It is no wonder that Simos is considered to be one of the best beaches on Elafonissos Island. In fact the beach is considered to be one of the top beaches in Greece. Simos Beach can be reach by car. Simos actually consists of two beaches, Megalos (Large) Simos and Mikros (Small) Simos. Megalos Simos is the longest beach on Elafonissos. Mikros Simos beach is just a short walk away. A narrow stretch of white sand divides these two magnificent beaches which are gifted with turquoise exotic clear clean seawater. The area is made up of white sand dunes and crystal clear seawater that offer the visitor a unique swimming experience. When the weather is windy, Simos is ideal for windsurfing as well. It is one of the best-organised beaches on Elafonissos with sunbeds, umbrellas, beach bars and a couple of tavernas nearby. During high season, it can get very crowded…

Greece at its Best

Paleokastritsa Village and Beach on the Island of Corfu

Paleokastritsa is arguably the most famous picturesque village on the Island of Corfu and is located 25 km northwest of Corfu Town. The word Paleokastritsa literally means old fortress, witnessing to the existence of a castle on the rocky cove before it was replaced by the Monastery of the Virgin. The village of Paleokastritsa offers a plethora of local taverns overlooking the blue bay and six sandy and pebbled beaches which are scattered all around the coves of Paleokastritsa. Those beaches are surrounded by olive tree forests creating a vista of dramatic yet beautiful scenery. This cosmopolitan resort stretches along a coastal road around stunning bays and a picturesque harbour where the excursion boats depart for some of the nearby isolated beaches. The settlement itself retains its traditional charm and character but can be very busy in high season. It is considered to be one of the main tourist attractions on the Island of Corfu. Passed the main harbour is the Monastery of the Virgin which dominates the village. The monastery hosts an interesting collection of post Byzantine icons, books and many other objects of interest. The main beach of Paleokastritsa is quite small but extremely well known for its cold clear sea and delightful environment. Paleokastritsa is considered to be one of the best beaches in the Greek Islands. It is surrounded by lovely scenery and offers the visitor some excellent sea views…

Greece at its Best

Greek Cities, Towns and Villages

Apart from beautiful beaches, Greece also has traditional and picturesque villages. These villages have differences in architecture, depending on their geographical location. Villages in Cyclades are famous for the white sugar houses, villages in Dodecanese have a medieval style, and towns and villages on the mainland have more earthy colours, while many Greek cities have beautiful Neo-classical buildings. Villages in the Cyclades group of Islands are usually constructed around a port or along the slopes of a hill with breathtaking sea view. Houses are small and have courtyards that are full of flowers. You will see no large blocks of flats on these Islands. The houses have window shutters and doors which are usually painted in blue or other vibrant colours. Churches have white walls and blue domes, while the streets in the village centres are narrow and paved. The capital towns of the Cycladic Islands are usually called Chora. The most famous village in Greece is Oia. Which is located on the Cycladic Island of Santorini. The Old Towns of Rhodes and Corfu are characteristic examples of this architecture with two or three storey residences, no balconies and paved streets. Similar old towns are found on other Island such as Chania, Rethymno and Heraklion on Crete and on the mainland at Monemvasia and Nafplion in the Peloponnese region of Greece. There are also many Venetian Castles found all around the mainland of the country and also on the Greek Islands. The more traditional style found in the mountain villages which have small stone houses, lovely yards and paved central squares. Due to their remote location, mountainous villages have few inhabitants. Pelion, Zagoria and the Peloponnese are among the Greek regions that have very picturesque villages in the mountains. Most of the people who live in these villages make their living from agriculture and cattle-breeding, while seaside villages mainly rely on the income that tourism brings them…

Greece at its Best

Where to go in Greece

One of the hardest tasks facing any visitor to Greece is to decide where to go and where to stay. There are so many beautiful places in Greece with so many wonderful ancient sites, cities, towns, villages and beach resorts to choose from. What follows, is just a few that, I believe, are amongst the best locations that Greece has to offer.

The Village of Oia on the Island of Santorini

Oia is located on the northern side of the Island of Santorini and is the most beautiful village on the Island. The village is world famous for its romantic sunsets, the picturesque architecture, the blue domed churches and the fabulous view to the Aegean Sea. The village of Oia is a favourite location for artists and couples. In fact, many weddings take place here every year. Although this is the most popular spot on Santorini, Oia has managed to keep intact its romantic and authentic feel and style.

Rhodes Town on the Island of Rhodes

Rhodes Town is among the best preserved Venetian towns in Europe. Located on the northern side of the Island of Rhodes, it is very busy both by day and by night. The old part of the town is certainly the most beautiful quarter with tall Venetian buildings, old churches, the Palace of the Grand Master, the Street of the Knights and the picturesque port of Mandraki…

Greece at its Best

Mykonos Town on the Island of Mykonos

Mykonos Town, also known as Chora, is the capital and centre of activities on the Greek Island of Mykonos. The village is famous for its sugar white houses, the paved streets, the picturesque harbour of Little Venice and the bars that stay open all night long. Walking around Mykonos Town, you may see the famous Peter the pelican, who will also be wandering around. Buses and boats from Mykonos Town go to various beaches on the Island.

Corfu Town on the Island of Corfu

Corfu Town is one of the most beautiful towns in Greece. Corfu Town stands out for its wonderful Venetian style of buildings and the romantic atmosphere that percolates around the old part of town. The architecture of Corfu has been greatly influenced by the architecture of Italian towns, like Venice and Florence. The Old Town of Corfu is the most impressive part. It has two fortresses that protected the Island of Corfu from pirates or enemies in medieval times, many churches, paved paths and two or three storey Venetian buildings still exist in the town. The most impressive places to visit are the Liston Avenue and the large Spianada Square…

Greece at its Best

Plaka in the Greek Capital City of Athens

Plaka is actually the historical centre of Athens. Plaka is a short walk away from the city centre and right under the tourist hot spot of the Acropolis. Plaka has a nice, relaxing feeling away from the noisy crowds. The area is crossed by paved paths and has lovely Neo-classical buildings to look at. It really is a nice quarter to stroll around the shops, enjoy a coffee (you should always find time for a coffee) or have dinner in the many traditional tavernas of the area. Geographically Plaka is bordered by the Roman Agora in Monastiraki, the Arch of Hadrian and the Acropolis Museum…

Greece at its Best

The Port of Fiscardo on the Island of Kefalonia

Located on the northern side of the Island of Kefalonia, Fiscardo stretches around a lovely port. Surrounded by lush greenery, this is one of the most popular mooring ports for private yachts in the Ionian Sea. The port promenade of Fiscardo is lined with many good fish taverns, cafeterias and lounge bars, making it a popular place to be seen in all day and night. Close to Fiscardo there are some nice coves for swimming and diving. The port of Fiscardo is linked by ferry to the Islands of Lefkada and Ithaca…

Greece at its Best

The Village of Apiranthos on the Island of Naxos

Located in the centre of the Island of Naxos, the name of this village literally means plenty of flowers. Apiranthos is surrounded by green mountains and stands out for its traditional architecture. The village has four museums and a beautiful central square, this is a wonderful place to stroll around and meet the authentic friendly Greek people of Naxos. There are many Venetian towers in Apiranthos from the medieval era in the village…

Greece at its Best

The Village of Olympos in the Karpathos region of Greece

Located on the northern side of the Karpathos Mountains, Olympos is a truly unique village. Surrounded by wild mountains, it seems, at times, like the village is lost in the clouds. Due to its isolate location and being away from the tourist crowds, the locals have managed to keep their original character: women wear their traditional custom every day and each house has an outdoors wooden oven and a small chapel in the yard. This really is a step back in time…

Greece at its Best

The Medieval Castle of Monemvasia in the Peloponnese

The Medieval Castle of Monemvasia is among the few castles that is still inhabited in Greece. The town is located on a small Island off the east coast of the Peloponnese region of Greece. The Medieval Castle (Kastro) of Monemvasia is divided into two quarters: Ano Poli (Upper Town) Town and Kato Poli (Lower Town). Kato Poli has shops, restaurants and old residences now turned into boutique hotels, while Ano Poli is not inhabited. From the top of the Castle, visitors get a breathtaking view to the mountains, coast and of the sea beyond…

Greece at its Best

The Village of Makrinitsa in the Pelion Region of Greece

The village of Makrinitsa is situated in the north western part of the Pelion Mountains, 6 km northeast of Volos. The mountainous region of Pelion has many wonderful villages with traditional stone houses and paved paths, surrounded by lush greenery. Makrinitsa stands out for its lovely central square with a gorgeous view all the way to the town of Volos and the Pagasetic Gulf beyond. Visitors love walking around the paved streets and checking out the traditional products for sale at the entrance path to the village of Makrinitsa. The surrounding countryside is gorgeous and many hiking trails start from or cross this beautiful village…

Greece at its Best

Skiathos Town on the Island of Skiathos

Skiathos Town is the capital of the Island of Skiathos and is built amphitheatrically on the south eastern tip of the Island in a windless bay, full of simple white houses with tiled roofs and narrow streets. Because the town was destroyed by German bombs during World War II, it was rebuilt and has since prospered. Today almost the entire population of Skiathos is concentrated in the town. Skiathos Town has plenty of restaurants (Greek and international cuisine), tourist offices, shops (touristy, clothes and shoe shops), cafes and tavernas. Most of the shops are located on the main street called Papadiamanti with most of the tavernas and restaurants on the seafront. In the town snack bars can be found in great quantity as well as luxurious restaurant such as Italian or there is even a Greek restaurant functioning in a renovated windmill which is located on the highest hill of the town, overlooking the sea and the Islands port. The commercial port is separated from the old port by the little peninsula of Bourtzi, covered with verdant pine trees. On this peninsula are the remains of the old castle built by the Gizi brothers during the Venetian period. The old port is very picturesque and is a pleasant place for a walk. The old port has several traditional little fishing boats bobbing up and down in the harbour. Susie and I love this place. As we have seen there is so much that is Best about Greece and in the next chapter we will consider the things that make up **Being Greek**…

Being Greek

Almost since time began Greece has been recognised as the birthplace of civilisation and democracy. Athens is one of the oldest cities in Europe. Greece and Athens in particular is also seen as the birthplace of democracy, Western philosophy, the Olympic Games, political science, Western literature, historiography, major mathematical principles, and Western theories of tragedy and comedy. Greece has given man its Gods of Mythology, the Olympic Games, The Parthenon (see above), Minoan Culture and much, much more. In more recent times it has been the country of choice for a vast number of visitors (tourists) both to see its ancient cultural heritage sites, cities and to visit its multitude of paradise Islands. Greece has an abundance of fabulous beaches, rugged scenery and a very warm, welcoming and friendly people…

Being Greek

Susie and Alan at Troulos Bay Hotel on the Island of Skiathos

Susie and I have spent many a happy summer holiday on one of the many Greek Islands as well as being lucky enough to have been able to visit many of the important ancient sites and cities on the mainland of Greece over the last twenty five years. During our many holidays to Greece we have met and befriended many of the local Greek people. We have, over the years, been told by our Greek hosts many interesting facts about Greece, its customs and its people. We have found these facts interesting and enlightening. They help to explain many of things about the ways of the Greeks that we did not understand. I have therefore, included these facts in the pages that follow so you too can begin to understand what it is all about "**Being Greek**"…

Being Greek

Frappe Time…

Greece has an area of 50,949 square miles (131,958 square kilometres), Greece is roughly the size of Alabama. The population of Greece is more than 10 million people.

Greece attracts approximately 16.5 million tourists each year which is more than the country's entire population. Tourism constitutes nearly 16% of the Gross Domestic Product (GDP) of Greece.

In Greece everyone has to vote. Voting is required by law for every citizen who is 18 years of age or older.

About 7% of all the marble produced in the world comes from Greece.

Greece has more international airports than most other countries in the world. This is because there are so many foreign tourists that want to visit its shores.

Greece is the world's third leading producer of olives. The Greeks have cultivated olive trees since ancient times. Some olive trees planted in the thirteenth century are still producing olives today…

Being Greek

According to Greek mythology, Athena and Poseidon agreed that whoever gave the city of Athens the best gift would become guardian over the city. Though Poseidon gave the gift of water, Athena's gift of an olive tree was deemed by the other gods to be more valuable and so she became guardian of the city of Athens.

It is a fact that Greece has zero navigable rivers this is because of the mountainous terrain. Nearly 80% of Greece is mountainous.

In Greece approximately 98% of the people are ethnic Greeks. Turks form the largest minority group. Other minorities are Albanians, Macedonians, Bulgarians, Armenians, and gypsies.

About 12 million people around the world speak Greek. They live mostly in Greece, Cyprus, Italy, Albania, Turkey and the United States of America, among other countries.

Thousands of English words come from the Greek language, sometimes via the Roman adaptation into Latin and then into English. Common English words from Greek include "academy," "apology," "marathon," "siren," "alphabet," and "typhoon."…

Being Greek

The Greek National costume…

In the 1950's, only about 30% of Greek adults could read and write. Now, the literacy rate is more than 95%.

An old Greek legend says that when God created the world, he sifted all the soil onto the earth through a strainer. After every country had good soil, he tossed the stones left in the strainer over his shoulder and that is what created Greece.

Greece has more than 2,000 islands, of which approximately 170 are populated. Greece's largest island is Crete (3,189 sq. miles) (8,260 sq. km.).

Over 40% of the population of Greece lives in the capital Athens (*Athina* in Greek). Since becoming the capital of modern Greece, its population has risen from 10,000 in 1834 to 3.6 million in 2001.

Greece has been continuously inhabited for over 7,000 years.

The Greek civilisation has been around for so long, that some would say, that it has had a chance to try nearly every form of government…

Being Greek

Greece enjoys more than 250 days of sunshine each year which means that they have 3,000 hours of sun every year.

Currently, Greek men must serve from one year to 18 months in a branch of the counties armed forces. The government spends 6% of the annual Gross Domestic Product (GDP) on the military.

Ancient Greece was not a single country like modern Greece. Rather, it was made up of about 1,500 different city-states or *poleis* (singular, *polis*). Each had its own laws and army, and they often quarrelled and waged war on one another. Athens was the largest city-state.

Until the late 1990's, the greatest threat to Greece was Turkey, as the two nations have had historical disputes over Cyprus and other territory for decades. After coming to each other's aid after a devastating earthquake that hit both countries in 1999, their relationship has improved.

Currently the life expectancy for Greek females is 82 years and for men, 77 years. Greece is ranked 26th in the world for life expectancy rates.

Greece is the leading producer of sea sponges in the world…

Being Greek

Football is the national sport of Greece.

Greek merchant ships make up 70% of the European Union's total merchant fleet. According to Greek law, 75% of a ship's crew must be Greek.

Greece has more archaeological museums than any other country in the world.

Retirement homes are rare in Greece. Grandparents usually live with their children's family until they die. Most young people live with their families until they marry.

Many Greek structures such as doors, windowsills, furniture, and church domes are painted a turquoise blue, especially in the Cyclades Islands. It is used because of an ancient belief that this shade of blue keeps evil away.

Feta cheese, which is made from goat's milk is the Greek's national cheese and dates back to the Homeric ages. The average per-capita consumption of feta cheese in Greece is the highest in the world…

Being Greek

In Greece, people celebrate the "name day" of the saint that bears their name rather than their own birthday.

Thousands of birds stop in Greece's wetlands on their migrations. As many as 100,000 birds from northern Europe and Asia spend their winters there.

The saying "taking the bull by its horns" comes from the Greek myth of Hercules saving Crete from a raging bull by seizing its horns.

The city of Rhodes (the capital of the island of Rhodes) is famous for housing one of the Seven Wonders of the Ancient World: the Colossus of Rhodes (from which the word "colossal" is derived). This gigantic 98-foot (303-meter) statue of the god Helios, whose legs straddled the harbour, unfortunately was destroyed by an earthquake in 226 B.C.

The first Olympic Games took place in 776 B.C. The first Greek Olympic champion was a Greek cook named Coroebus who won the sprint race…

Being Greek

Monk Seal…

Slaves made up between 40% and 80% of ancient Greece's population. Slaves were captives from wars, abandoned children, or children of slaves.

A long-standing dispute between Britain and Greece concerns the Elgin Marbles (the Greeks prefer to call them the Parthenon Marbles), which are housed in a London museum. The British government believes that it acquired them fairly through its purchase from Lord Elgin, while the Greeks claim the purchase was illegal as the marbles were the property of the Greek people and therefore, stolen.

Greece has one of the richest diversities of wildlife in Europe, including 116 species of mammals, 18 of amphibians, 59 of reptiles, 240 of bird, and 107 of fish. However, about half of the endemic mammal species are currently in danger of becoming extinct.

The monk seal has been a part of Greek's natural and cultural heritage and is described in **The Odyssey**. The head of a monk seal was even found on a coin dated 500 BC…

Being Greek

Alexander the Great **Aristotle**

Greece organized the first municipal rubbish/waste dump in the Western world in around 500 B.C.

During the Nazi occupation of Greece in WWII, most Jews were taken to concentration camps across Europe. The Jewish population in Greece fell sharply from 78,000 to less than 13,000 by the end of the war.

In Greece, the dead are always buried because the Greek Orthodox Church forbids cremation. Five years after a burial, the body is exhumed and the bones are first washed with wine and then placed in an ossuary. This is done in part to relieve the shortage of land available in Greek cemeteries.

Government corruption cost Greece about $1 billion in 2009. Currently Greece's national debt is larger than the country's economy. Its credit rating, or its perceived ability to repay debts, is the lowest in the euro zone.

The Greek language has been spoken for more than 3,000 years, making it one of the oldest languages in Europe…

Being Greek

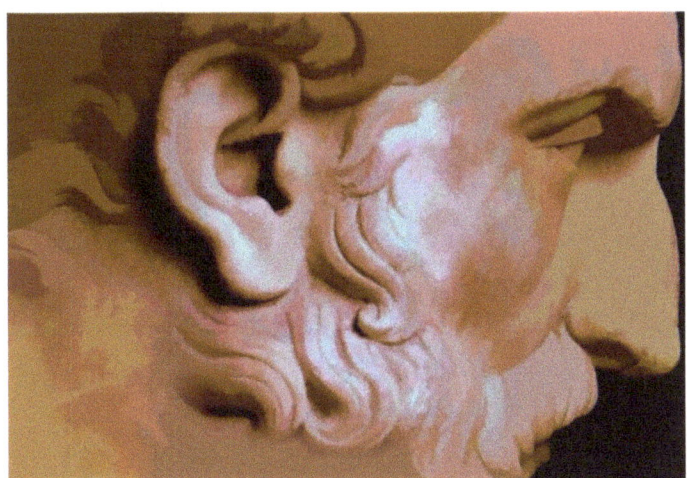

Epicurus…

Greeks do not wave with an open hand. In fact, it is considered an insult to show the palm of the hand with the fingers extended. Greeks wave with the palm closed.

After giving a compliment, Greeks make a puff of breath through pursed lips, as if spitting. This is meant to protect the person receiving the compliment from the "evil eye".

No point in Greece is more than 85 miles (137 kilometres) from seawater. Greece has about 9,000 miles of coastline, the 10th longest coastline in the world.

Greece was once a mass of rock that was completely underwater. When a tectonic plate crashed into Europe, the collision raised the sea bed and created Greece's mountain ranges. The plate is still moving and causes earthquakes and tremors all around the Aegean most years.

Soldiers (*hoplites*) in ancient Greece soldiers wore up to 70 pounds (33 kilograms) of bronze armour…

Being Greek

Socrates

Plato

The first historian in the world is considered to be the Greek writer Herodotus (c. 484-425 B.C.), the author of the first great book of history on the Greco-Persian Wars.

The ancient Greeks are often called the inventors of mathematics because they were the first to make it a theoretical discipline. The work of Greek mathematicians such as Pythagoras, Euclid, Archimedes, and Apollonius lies at the basis of modern mathematics.

The first Greek philosopher is considered to be Thales of Miletus (c. 624-546 B.C.). He was the first to give a natural explanation of the origin of the world rather than a mythological one.

The Peloponnesian War (431-404 B.C.) between Athens and the Peloponnesian League led by Sparta left ancient Greece in ruins and marked the end of the golden age of Greece.

A Spartan specialty was a black soup made from salt, vinegar, and blood. No one in the rest of Greece would drink it…

Being Greek

Greek Tragedy Masks

The British poet Lord Byron (1788-1824) was so enamoured with the Greeks that he travelled to Greece to fight against the Turks in the Greek War of Independence. He contracted a fever there and died at the age of 36. The Greeks consider him a national hero.

The word "barbarian" comes from Greek barbaroi, which means people who do not speak Greek and therefore sound like they're saying "bar-bar-bar-bar."

In ancient Greece one of the dishes enjoyed by ancient Greek men at feasts was roast pig stuffed with thrushes, ducks, eggs, and oysters. Most feasts were for men only, though there were female entertainers (this was not however, considered a respectable occupation for a women).

The first Greek tragedy was performed in 534 B.C. and was staged by a priest of Dionysus named Thespis. He also wrote and performed a part separate from the traditional tragic chorus, which also designated him as the first actor. In fact, the word "thespian" (actor) derives from his name…

Being Greek

Spartan Warriors

At its height, Greek colonisation reached as far as Russia and France to the west and Turkey to the Far East.

Pre-Socratic Greek philosopher Anaximander (c. 610-546 B.C.) is credited with writing the first philosophical treatise and making the first map of the known world. He can also be considered the first scientist who recorded a scientific experiment.

Spartan warriors were known for their long, flowing hair. Before a battle, they would carefully comb it. Cowardly soldiers would have half their hair and half their beards shaved off.

In ancient Greece wealthy people would sacrifice animals at the temples. Poor people who couldn't afford live animals offered pastry ones instead.

Ostracism allowed Athenian citizens to temporarily exile people who were thought dangerous to the public. If it was voted that ostracism was necessary, each citizen inscribed a name on a piece of pottery or ostracon in a secret ballet. The person with the most votes had to leave town within 10 days for 10 years…

Being Greek

Democritus

Heraclitus

Only boys and men were actors in ancient Greek plays. They wore large masks so audience members could see what part they were playing. Theatre staff carried big sticks to control the audience because sometimes the huge audiences would get over excited by a play and would riot.

The term "Ancient Greece" usually refers to the time between Homer (c. 750 B.C.) and the Roman conquest of Ptolemaic Egypt (Antony and Cleopatra, 30 B.C.).

Democracy in Athens was significantly different from modern democracies in that it was both more participatory and exclusive. There were also no political parties in Athenian democracy.

The Greeks, in ancient times, would sacrifice one hundred bulls to Zeus during each Olympic Games.

The Greeks revolutionised the art of sculpture. Instead of stiff poses and blank faces, Greek artists began to carve statues of people that showed both movement and emotion…

Being Greek

The Greek Temple of Artemis

The Greek Temple of Artemis, built on the site of two earlier shrines dating back as far as the eight century B.C. in modern-day Turkey, was one of the Seven Wonders of the Ancient World. It was built around 550 B.C. and was destroyed in 356 B.C. by Herostratus.

The Parthenon (Place of the Partheons, from parthenos or "virgin") was built almost 2,500 years ago and sits on the Acropolis above the city of Athens. It actually featured colourful sculptures and a large gold-and-ivory statue of Athena. It took 15 years to build.

The ancestors of the Greeks were Indo-Europeans who entered Greece around 1900 B.C. They lived alongside the Minoans for many centuries before giving rise to the Mycenaean civilization which ended abruptly in the twelfth century B.C. After a "dark ages" of 300 years in which the knowledge of writing was lost, Greece gave birth to one of the most influential civilisation the world has ever known: Classical Greece.

By law, the only people eligible for citizenship in Sparta were direct descendants of the original Doric settlers. Because of this, there were never more than about 6,000-7,000 male citizens in Sparta, compared with up to 40,000 in Athens…

Being Greek

Mount Olympus

Greek's highest elevation is the legendary home of Zeus and other Olympian gods and goddesses, Mount Olympus at 9,750 feet (2,917 meters). Its lowest elevation is the Mediterranean Sea, or sea level.

Alexander the Great was the first Greek ruler to put his own face on Greek coins. Previously, Greek coins had shown the face of a god or goddess.

The word "tragedy" is Greek for "goat-song" because early Greek tragedies honoured Dionysus, the god of wine, and the players wore goatskins. Tragedies were noble stories of gods, kings, and heroes. Comedy or "revel," on the other hand, were about lower-class characters and their antics.

The most famous modern writer in Greece is Nikos Kazantzakis (1883-1957). His novels **Zorba the Greek** and **The Last Temptation of Christ** were both made into movies, though the Greek Orthodox Church expelled him for **The Last Temptation of Christ**.

Greece's official name is the Hellenic Republic. It is also known as Ellas or Ellada…

Being Greek

The Greek flag includes nine blue-and-white horizontal stripes, which some scholars say stand for the nine syllables of the Greek motto "Eleftheria i Thanatos" or "Freedom or Death." Blue represents Greece's sea and sky, while white stands for the purity of the struggle of freedom. In the upper left-hand corner is the traditional Greek Orthodox cross.

Greece today has two major political parties: the Socialists (Panhellenic Socialists Movements or PASOK) and the Democrats (the New Democracy Party). Both were founded in 1974 after Greece's military dictatorship collapsed.

Greece has one of the lowest divorce rates in the EU (4.8% in 2016). Greece traditionally also has the highest abortion rates.

About 10% of a Greek worker's pay is taken for taxes and another 10% for national health care in return the government provides free hospitals and other medical services.

Greek workers currently get at least one month paid vacation every year…

Being Greek

About 10% of Greek adults are unemployed. Even with a college education, it's hard to find a job in Greece today.

Greece's previous currency, the drachma, was 2,650 years old and Europe's oldest currency. The drachma was replaced with the Euro in 2002.

Throughout history, Greeks have loved the sea. They have more than 1,800 merchant ships in service currently. Greece has one of the largest merchant shipping fleets in the world. Aristotle Onassis and Stavros Niarchos ("The Golden Greek") are some of the best-known Greek shipping businessmen.

When the Roman Empire split in two in A.D. 285, the eastern half, including Greece, became known as the Byzantine Empire. In 1453, Greece fell to the Ottoman Empire. Greece wouldn't achieve independence until 1829.

Greece is the European country with the largest number of newspapers. There are 18 daily newspapers in Athens. Foreign papers can also be found in large cities and on popular holiday Islands…

Being Greek

Roadside Shrine…

The Electricity supply in Greece is 220 volts AC, 50Hz. Round two-pin plugs are used. North American visitors require a transformer and British visitors an adaptor.

The time in Greece is like most other counties in Europe, Summer (Daylight-Saving) Time is observed in Greece, where the time is shifted forward by 1 hour; 3 hours ahead of Greenwich Mean Time (GMT+3). After the summer months the time in Greece is shifted back by 1 hour to Eastern European Time (EET) or (GMT+2).

In Greece the working hours for Banks and Public Services work are from 08.00 to 14.00, Monday to Friday. The shops are usually open Monday-Wednesday-Saturday from 09.00 to 15.00 and Tuesday-Thursday-Friday from 09.00 to 14.00 and 17.00 to 20.00. In these three days of the week, shops close for the siesta at noon and open again in the afternoon. In the tourist areas in high season, most shops stay open all day long, from early in the morning till late in the evening. Malls in the cities also stay open all day.

Anyone who has visited Greece will be well aware of the numerous small roadside shrines that often contain lit candles and vases of dried flowers. These are erected at sites where loved ones have had a tragic accident, often fatal and their family leave them a lighted candle to remember them…

Being Greek

The Greek Transport Team!…

Driving in Greece: For those of you that have already sampled the delights of driving on Greek roads you will be familiar with the sometimes unfinished state of the road surface and of the sides of the road and ditches being full of builder's rubble and litter. Beside many of the main roads you will see large advertising boards touting brands of cigarettes, coffee and/or sporting goods.

Greek time: In the summertime, Greece is two hours ahead of the time in the UK (Greenwich meridian time) like elsewhere in Europe. Also in Greece, in the summer season (March – September) you will find that there is something very curious about time. In Greece it is conceived in a very particular way. Here time is not running, there is no such concept of "being on time or late" and a watch is just something to wear. The Greeks themselves are aware of the need for them to take it easy (but not in serving the tourist!) up to the point that G.M.T. is not considered as the Greenwich Meridian Time, but as the Greek Maybe Time! So remember you are on holiday take your time and relax things will get done in the fullness of time or should I say in Greek time.

Religious festivals: Throughout Greece, religious festivals have become a true backbone to many communities. All kinds of festivals and religious feast events take place for example Christian Holy events during Easter, when churches are covered with colourful flowers and bay leaves…

Being Greek

The rosary that most of the Greek men are holding in their hands, sitting outside the kafeneion (cafe in Greece), has no religious meaning, but is only a way of killing time. Try and buy one, it's actually much more difficult to swing it than it looks.

The iron bars sticking out from the flat Greek house roof are exclusively there for the purpose of a later extension to the house. They have **NOTHING** to do with exemptions from taxpaying, as long as the house isn't yet finished. (It is a good story though)!

On an Olive tree the trunks of the trees are often painted white (lime-wash) in Greece. It is used primarily to fight ants and besides it looks nice, too!

A single person sitting at a taverna, can wait quite a long time for the waiter to show up. In Greece it's very unlikely that anybody eats alone. He/she must be waiting for someone. For the waiter it will be very impolite and bumptious, to ask for the order before all the guests have arrived. This has changed in the major tourist places, and especially for tourists, but you can still run into this phenomenon in the villages of many places in Greece…

Being Greek

When the Greeks go out for dinner, they always pay cash. NO cheque's and credit cards! And they have always got money enough to pay the bill for their company too. Not being able to pay, would be humiliating beyond belief.

Unfinished buildings is a common sight in Greece. The reason is that Greek people build what they need today and leave the rest of the building unfinished for the future. It may seem that the Greeks are constantly building houses - and they are. Most Greek parents build a house for each daughter, but not for their sons (as they are supposed to marry a girl who will get a house from her parents). Often it is also the daughter that inherits her parents' or grandparents' house when they die.

You might get the impression that Greek men always sit in cafes and drink. They do often go to a kafeneion, but not always, and rarely for a very long time. Often they have a cup of Greek coffee only. Most of them stay there for a short time, just enough to hear what has happened and also to make an appointment with for example the local electrician or the local bricklayer. Of course, Greek women can go to the kafeneion as well, but most of them don't want to, and besides they hear all the gossip from the husband when he comes home. For about 20 years ago, you would always find at least two kafenions in a village, no matter how small it was, but painted in different colours. The colours indicated the political party of the owner of the kafenion. This way you avoided political quarrels. Rather practical! It can still be found, but it has become more and more rare as less and less people care about politics in Greece today…

Being Greek

Theft is very, very rare in Greece. It's simply considered too humiliating to steel other people's things or money. On the other hand it's OK to cheat a bit - especially if they don't like the person they cheat.

You will see a Greek priest - or pappas, as they are called - everywhere, as you cannot miss them in their long, black dress and high hat. They are not obliged to wear their priest clothes all the time, but they do, as it is most practical and they are easier to identify this way.

Greek priests can marry and have children, just like in the Lutheran church. But you will never see a woman priest. This is not allowed by the Greek Orthodox Church.

At most beaches you will have to pay for a sun bed and an umbrella. If you think that it is just people trying to get money out of the tourists you're very wrong. It's a job in Greece having a piece of a beach. A man bids for a particular part of the beach each year, and he pays a sum of money, to be allowed to put up his sun beds and umbrellas. During the season it is his responsibility that this part of the beach is kept properly. The price you pay will depend on where the beach is situated, what kind of facilities like a taverna, toilets and/or showers there are. The tourist police checks that he does his job properly…

Being Greek

If you want to see a Greek Church or monastery inside, you must be properly dressed. It's considered rude to enter a church if your shoulders and knees aren't covered. This rule goes for both men and women. So if you are a tourist and wants to be polite in the country you are visiting then please dress respectfully when visiting a church.

If a Greek invites you out for dinner or a drink, don't **EVER** try to make him "split the bill in half" as we often do here in Northern Europe. I know some tourists who have wanted to be nice to their host for the evening, and they snapped the bill out of his hand and paid it. Never has a friendship been that close to ruin, and the Greek man was more embarrassed than you could ever imagine!

If you are invited to a Greek home, remember to bring something for the hosts. Flowers or chocolate is the most common. If the occasion is a name day, you must bring a present, which you deliver when you enter the house. The present will be put together with the rest of the presents on a table - unopened. The Greeks will open the gifts when all the guests have left. If he or she doesn't like the gift they don't have to pretend and show a lot of gratitude that they really do not feel. Actually it is a very practical habit.

Officially there is equality between the sexes, but still in Greece today women are often paid less then men…

Being Greek

About 40 % of the Greek women are engaged in active employment.

Theoretically Greek women are liable for military service, but only volunteers are taking part in the service, and the women seem to be satisfied with this situation.

When divorcing, all belongings are equally split between the man and woman.

Today a Greek woman may keep her maiden name when marrying.

Today Greek women only give birth to half as many children, as they did before World War 2. The Greek birth-rate is the second lowest in Europe. Italy has the lowest birth-rate.

Since 1982 it has been legal to have a civil marriage. But still 95 % are married religiously in the church.

Arranged marriages are forbidden by law. Paying dowry is illegal too. But still there are examples of both these happening today especially in the villages…

Being Greek

Bullet holes in road signs. It is no secret that Greeks own guns, especially in mountainous areas. Road signs are easy targets and you will see many of them that resemble Swiss cheese after suffering some shooting practice. Greeks also usually fire their guns at weddings and other celebrations.

Churches (ekklisies): Big churches are usually found inside the towns but the numerous small ones are practically everywhere. Usually they are white-painted, you will find them on a beach, on the mountain peaks, in deep gorges or inside caves. The people of Greece are deeply religious people and they build churches to express their gratitude to God or to fulfil a "tama", a promise given to God in exchange for a request. The miniature churches next to the roads however, are memorials for people killed in a car accident, at the same spot where the accident happened. The family of the deceased construct and maintain them. They contain a photo of the deceased, some religious objects and a lit candle.

Erotas or Eros, son of Aphrodite, was a god in ancient Greece: It is difficult to give the meaning of the Greek word "erotas" because there is no word for it in English. The closest translation is "being in love". The English word Love is "Agapi" in Greek…

Being Greek

Erontas or diktamos is the Greek name for the herb dittany: It used to be a rare, hard to collect herb because it grew on steep cliffs in mountainous areas. Today it is cultivated, so it has become easy to find. It is said that its name "erontas", which is actually the same word as erotas, was given to it because a man should be deeply in love with a woman in order to risk his life to collect it for her from a steep cliff.

Fresh fish in Greece has become rare and quite expensive. Common fish that you will find at restaurants are: red mullet, sea bream, red snapper, swordfish and tuna. octopus, squids, shrimps and mussels are also easy to find and they taste great. Fish like sand-smelt or silverside are quite cheap and tasty, although its taste is described as "fishy" by people who are not used to Mediterranean fish.

Garides are shrimps (see above): Have them grilled, boiled or "saganaki" with tomatoes and feta cheese…

Being Greek

A Greek Salad (see above): In Greek it is called "horiatiki" and it is a tasty salad made from fresh tomatoes, cucumber, olives and feta cheese. Add some oregano, vinegar and plenty of Greek olive oil and you have a tasty and fulfilling dish.

Herbs: If I had to describe Greece in just five words only, then I would choose: sun, sea, mountains, sage and thyme. Sage and thyme are everywhere in Greece and the air is full of their characteristic smell. Herbs have been used for ages by the people of Greece as medicines. Try a tea of camomile and sage if you have a sore throat. If you do not like the taste you can add some honey to it. If your nose is blocked and you cannot breathe easily, then have a tea made from thyme.

Honey of excellent quality is produced in Greece. Thyme honey is considered to be the best.

Immigrants: Albanians, Bulgarians, Russians, Ukranian and others from Eastern Europe have moved to Greece in big numbers. Most of them work in agriculture and construction and their number is now more than 10% of the Greek population. They adjusted quickly to the Greek way of life and their children go to Greek schools…

Being Greek

Kafeneio, the Greek café (see above): Is a very important part of the social life of all parts of Greece. Greeks will often tell you that you should always find the time for a cup of coffee.

Lamb meat: The best meat you can have in Greece is the young lamb or young goat meat from animals raised in the mountainous areas. If you happen to be in a taverna in a small mountainous village, ask them for grilled paidakia.

Mizithra: A fresh soft white cheese. It contains lower fat and cholesterol than yellow cheese is made from sheep's milk.

Paximadi: The traditional Greek way of preserving bread for a long time. It is hard dried bread that gets soft when you add some water to it. You will find it in various forms, sizes and made from wheat or barley, with or without yeast, whole grain or not. Pour some olive oil on a big round piece of paximadi, add some grated tomato, oregano and feta cheese and you will have the very tasty appetizer.

Pita Giros are slices of grilled pork meat with yoghurt, lots of onion, French fries, salt and pepper, all wrapped inside a round "pita" bread. Pita - giros is the fast food of Greece and you can find it almost everywhere. Chicken giros is becoming popular lately because of the smaller amount of fat that it contains…

Being Greek

Plane Tree…

Souvlaki…

Platanos or Plane Tree (see above): A tree that grows close to water. You can find it usually close to a river in gorges or in the central square of villages in Greece. It looks similar to the maple tree and it can grow very big.

Sariki: Is the traditional head covering for the men of Crete. It is black and is wrapped many times around the top of the head.

Souvlaki (see above) is skewered pork meat, a traditional Greek dish. It is served with French fries and there is also chicken, lamb and swordfish souvlaki…

Being Greek

We love Troulos Bay on the Greek Island of Skiathos

Vegetables. Greece produces many different kinds of vegetables and they taste a lot better than what you will find in the supermarkets in the rest of Europe.

Xanthies: blonde tourist women (see above). Highly appreciated by the "kamakia", the young hot-blooded Greek lovers. Love stories between the men of Greece and female tourists are common each year. Most of them are just summer love but a few marriages come out of them. The result is that there are many European women living in Greece, mostly German, Dutch and Scandinavian. Be aware though, that having a romantic love affair during your holiday is one thing and living in Greece married to a Greek man is totally another. The cultural differences are many and it is important not to ignore them.

Zucchini or Courgette. Try zucchini slices deep fried in olive oil. Fried aubergine slices are very tasty too.

Yannis and Yorgos, are the two most common names for men in Greece. Yannis is John and Yorgos is George. More common names are Manolis and Nikos. For women the most common name is Maria.

Now that we understand a bit more about what it is "Being Greek" it is time for us, in the final chapter, to enjoy seeing **Greece in full Colour**…

Greece in Colour

Alan waiting for his tea in Skiathos Town

Boats in harbour on the Island of Aegina

Greece in Colour

The Island of Alonissos

The Island of Amorgo and Greek cat on patrol

Greece in Colour

Chapel on the Island of Anafi

The Island of Andros and the curious Greek cat

Greece in Colour

The Acropolis of Athens

Cats on the Island of Skiathos

Greece in Colour

The Island of Corfu

The Bassae Temple of Apollo at Epicurius

Greece in Colour

Waves onto the Island of Crete

Cricket match on the Island of Corfu and cats feeding time

Greece in Colour

The Island of Crete

The Island of Evia

Greece in Colour

The Church at Folegandros

The Island of Evia

Greece in Colour

The Island of Hydra

The Island of Halki

Greece in Colour

The Island of Ikaria

Sunset on the Island of Ikaria

Greece in Colour

The Island of Ithaca

The Island of Kalymnos

Greece in Colour

Fiscardo on the Island of Kefalonia

Assos on the Island of Kefalonia and boats on the Island of Lesvos

Greece in Colour

Views of the Island of Kos

Greece in Colour

The Island of Lefkas

Sailing off the Island of Lemnos

Greece in Colour

The Island of Leros

The Island of Lesvos

Greece in Colour

Mending the nets on the Island of Lipsi

The Island of Meganissi

Greece in Colour

The Island of Meganissi

The Island of Mykonos

Greece in Colour

The Island of Mykonos

Ancient Site at Mystras

Greece in Colour

The Island of Naxos

The Island of Paros

Greece in Colour

Chapel on the Island of Patmos

The Island of Paxos

Greece in Colour

The Island of Poros

The Island of Rhodes

Greece in Colour

The Island of Samos

The Sanctuary of Apollo at Delphi

Greece in Colour

Taverna on the Island of Serifos

Windmill on the Island of Santorini

Greece in Colour

Church on the hill in Skiathos Town

Statue in the Old Port in Skiathos Town

Greece in Colour

Boats in the harbour on the Island of Spetses

Boat anchored off the Island of Symi

Greece in Colour

Church on the Island of Skopelos

Fishing boat coming into port on the Island of Skyros

Greece in Colour

The Island of Symi

Lighting the Olympic torch

Greece in Colour

Zakynthos Town

Boats anchored in Navro beach on the Island of Zakynthos

Greece in Colour

Greek dancers

Susie enjoying the sun on the Island of Kefalonia

Greece in Colour

Greek football fans

Greek flags flying proudly

Greece in Colour

Greek ancient bronze helmet and blue domed hillside church's

Taverna in Assos on Kefalonia and the Temple of Poseidon at Sounio

Greece in Colour

Greek priests

Greek Soldiers

Greece in Colour

Greek tragedy masks

Minoan's escaping from the volcano on the Island of Santorini

Greece in Colour

Shades on Thassos, Alan all at sea off Skiathos and the Island off Thassos

Greece in Colour

Windmills on the Island of Mykonos

Church on the Island of Patmos and flags on the Island of Santorini

Greece in Colour

Harbour on the Island of Skopelos

Houses on the Island of Symi and windmill on the Island of Santorini

Greece in Colour

Loggerhead turtle off the Island of Zakynthos

Shipwreck (Navro) beach on the Island of Zakynthos

Greece in Colour

Waving the planes in on the Island of Skiathos

The fantastic Troulos Bay Hotel on the Island of Skiathos

Greece in Colour

Alan is waving goodbye from the Troulos Bay Hotel on the Island of Skiathos

Susie and I Love Greece

After enjoying all of this beautiful colour I am sad to say that we have now reached the end of our journey together. There is just time for me to say a fond farewell and I hope that you have enjoyed our time together. So until the next time we meet, goodbye and I hope that you have the chance to visit this wonderful land of Greece and its kind, friendly and generous people real soon…

Acknowledgement

I would like to thank all the friendly people of Greece that Susie and I have met during our holidays on the mainland and on many of their beautiful Islands. A special mention must also go to our special holiday friends from Vienna Anna and Karl, Andrew and Lynn from Sheffield and Issy and Alistair from Scotland. I would also like to thank my publishers Rainbow Publications UK. For publishing this book and for giving me the opportunity for my writings to be read once more. Finally I wish to thank my wife Susie for her love and the support she gives me in all that I do every single day of my life.

Susie… 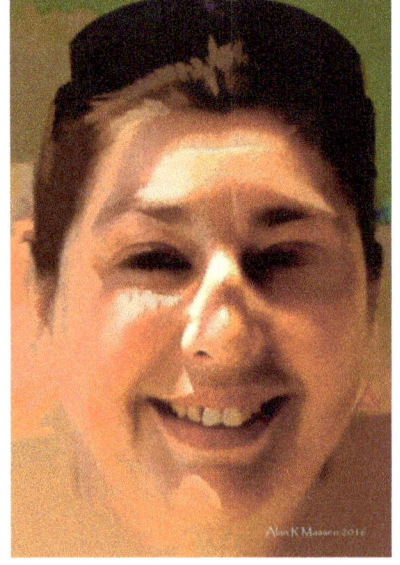  …Alan

Copyright © 2019 Alan R. Massen

I wish you all a very special

Thank You

www.ingramcontent.com/pod-product-compliance
Lightning Source LLC
Chambersburg PA
CBHW061926290426
44113CB00024B/2828